12 Sermons
on
Thanksgiving

Charles H. Spurgeon

BAKER
A DIVISION OF
Baker Book House Co

Reprinted 1994 by Baker Book House Company

Published by Baker Books
a division of Baker Book House Company
P.O. Box 6287, Grand Rapids, MI 49516-6287

Printed in the United States of America

ISBN 0-8010-8390-7

Reprinted from the edition issued by Passmore & Alabaster

Contents

1. Special Thanksgiving to the Father

"Giving thanks unto the Father, which hath made us meet to be partakers of the inheritance of the saints in light : who hath delivered us from the power of darkness, and hath translated us into the kingdom of his dear Son."—Col. i. 12, 13.

THIS passage is a mine of riches. I can anticipate the difficulty in preaching and the regret in concluding we shall experience this evening because we are not able to dig out all the gold which lies in this precious vein. We lack the power to grasp and the time to expatiate upon that volume of truths which is here condensed into a few short sentences.

We are exhorted to "give thanks unto the Father." This counsel is at once needful and salutary. I think, my brethren, we scarcely need to be told to give thanks unto the Son. The remembrance of that bleeding body hanging upon the cross is ever present to our faith. The nails and the spear, his griefs, the anguish of his soul, and his sweat of agony, make such tender touching appeals to our gratitude—these will prevent us always from ceasing our songs, and sometimes fire our hearts with rekindling rapture in praise of the *man* Christ Jesus. Yes, we *will* bless thee, dearest Lord; our souls are all on fire. As we survey the wondrous cross, we cannot but shout—

> " O for this love let rocks and hills
> Their lasting silence break,
> And all harmonious human tongues
> The Saviour's praises speak."

It is in a degree very much the same with the Holy Spirit. I think we are compelled to feel every day our dependence upon his constant influence. He abides with us as a present and personal Comforter and Counsellor. We, therefore, do praise the Spirit of Grace, who hath made our heart his temple, and who works in us all that is gracious, virtuous, and well-pleasing in the sight of God. If there be any one Person in the Trinity whom we are more apt to forget than another in our praises, it is God the Father. In fact there are some who even get a wrong idea of Him, a slanderous idea of that God whose name is LOVE, They imagine that love dwelt in Christ, rather than in the Father; and that our salvation is rather due to the Son and the Holy Spirit, than to our Father God. Let us not be of the number of the ignorant, but let us receive this truth. We are as much indebted to the Father as to any other Person of the Sacred Three. He as much and as truly loves us as any of the adorable Three Persons. He is as truly worthy of our highest praise as either the Son or the Holy Spirit.

A remarkable fact, which we should always bear in mind, is this:—in the Holy Scriptures most of the operations which are set down as being the works of the Spirit, are in other Scriptures ascribed to God the Father. Do we say it is God the Spirit that quickens the sinner who is dead in sin? it is true; but you will find in another passage it is said, "The Father quickeneth whom he will." Do we say that the Spirit is the sanctifier, and that the sanctification of the soul is wrought by the Holy Ghost? You will find a passage in the opening of the Epistle of St. Jude, in which it is said, "Sanctified by God the Father." Now, how are we to account for this? I think it may be explained thus. God the Spirit cometh from God the Father, and therefore whatever acts are performed by the Spirit are truly done by the Father, because he sendeth forth the Spirit. And again, the Spirit is often the instrument—though I say not this in any way to derogate from his glory—he is often the instrument with which the Father works. It is the Father who says to the dry bones, live; it is the Spirit who, going forth with the divine word, makes them live. The quickening is due as much to the word as to the influence that went with the word; and as the word came with all the bounty of free grace and goodwill from the Father, the quickening is due to him. It is true that the seal on our hearts is the Holy Spirit; he is the seal, but it is the Eternal Father's hand that stamps the seal; the Father communicates the Spirit to seal our adoption. The works of the Spirit are, many of them, I repeat it again, attributed to the Father, because he worketh in, through, and by the Spirit.

The works of the Son of God, I ought to observe are every one of them in intimate connection with the Father. If the Son comes into the world, it is because the Father sends him; if the Son calls his people, it is because his Father gave this people into his hands. If the Son redeems the chosen race, is not the Son himself the Father's gift, and doth not God send his Son into the world that we may live through him? So that the Father, the great Ancient of Days, is ever to be extolled; and we must never omit the full homage of our hearts to him when we sing that sacred doxology,

"Praise Father, Son, and Holy Ghost."

In order to excite your gratitude to God the Father to-night, I propose to dilate a little upon this passage, as God the Holy Spirit shall enable me. If you will look at the text, you will see two blessings in it. The first has regard to *the future*; it is a meetness for the inheritance of the saints in light. The second blessing, which must go with the first, for indeed it is the cause of the first, the effective cause, has relation to *the past*. Here we read of our deliverance from the power of darkness. Let us meditate a little upon each of these blessings, and then, in the third place, I will endeavour to show *the relation which exists between the two*.

I. The first blessing introduced to our notice is this—" God the Father has made us meet to be partakers of the inheritance of the saints in light." It is a PRESENT BLESSING. Not a mercy laid up for us in the covenant, which we have not yet received, but it is a blessing which every true believer already has in his hand. Those mercies in the covenant of which we have the earnest now while we wait for the full possession, are just as rich, and just as certain as those which have been already with abundant lovingkindness bestowed on us; but still they are not so precious in our enjoyment. The mercy we have in store, and in hand, is after all, the main source of our present comfort. And oh what a blessing this! "Made meet for the inheritance of the saints in light." The true believer is fit for heaven; he is meet to be a partaker of the inheritance—and that now, at this very moment. What does this mean? Does it mean that the believer is perfect; that he is free from sin? No, my brethren, where shall you ever find such perfection in this world? If no man can be a believer but the perfect man, then what has the perfect man to believe? Could he not walk by sight? When he is perfect, he may cease to be a believer. No, brethren, it is not such perfection that is meant, although perfection is implied, and assuredly will be given as the result. Far less does this mean that we have a right to eternal life from any doings of our own. We have a fitness for eternal life, a meetness for it, but we have no desert of it. We deserve nothing of God even now, in ourselves, but his eternal wrath and his infinite displeasure. What, then, does it mean? Why, it means just this: we are so far meet that we are accepted in the Beloved, adopted into the family, and fitted by divine approbation to dwell with the saints in light. There is a woman chosen to be a bride; she is fitted to be married, fitted to enter into the honourable state and condition of matrimony; but at present she has not on the bridal garment, she is not like the bride adorned for her husband. You do not see her yet robed in her elegant attire, with her ornaments upon her, but you know she is fitted to be a bride, she is received and welcomed as such in the family of her destination. So Christ has chosen his Church to be married to him; she has not yet put on her bridal garment, and all that beautiful array in which she shall stand before the Father's throne, but notwithstanding, there is such a fitness in her to be the bride of Christ, when she shall have bathed herself for a little while, and lain for a little while in the bed of spices—there is such a fitness in her character, such a grace-given adaptation in her to become the royal bride of her glorious Lord, and to become a partaker of the enjoyments of bliss—that it may be said of the church as a whole, and of every member of it, that they are "meet for the inheritance of the saints in light."

The Greek word, moreover, bears some such meaning as this, though I cannot give the exact idiom, it is always difficult when a word is not used often. This word is only used twice, that I am aware of, in the New Testament. The word may be employed for "suitable," or, I think, "sufficient." "He hath made us meet"—sufficient—" to be partakers of the inheritance of the saints in light." But I cannot give my idea without borrowing another figure. When a child is born, it is at once endowed with all the faculties of humanity. If those powers are awanting at first, they will not come afterwards. It has eyes, it has hands, it has feet, and all its physical organs. These of course are as it were in embryo. The senses though perfect at first, must be gradually developed, and the understanding gradually matured. It can see but little, it cannot discern distances; it can hear, but it cannot hear distinctly enough at first to know from what direction the sound comes; but you never find a new leg, a new arm, a new eye, or a new ear growing on that child. Each of these powers will expand and enlarge, but still there is the whole man there at first, and the child is *sufficient* for a man. Let but God in his infinite providence cause it to feed, and give it strength and increase, it has *sufficient* for manhood. It does not want either arm or leg, nose or ear; you cannot make it grow a new member; nor does it require a new member either; all are there. In like manner, the moment a man is regenerated, there is every faculty in his new creation that there shall be, even when he gets to heaven. It only needs to be developed and brought out: he will not have a new power, he will not have a new grace, he will have those which he had before, developed and brought out. Just as we are told by the careful observer, that in the acorn there is in embryo every root and every bough and every leaf of the future tree, which only requires to be developed and brought out in their fulness. So, in the true believer, there is a sufficiency or meetness for the inheritance of the saints in light. All that he requires is, not that a new thing should be implanted, but that that which God has put there in the moment of regeneration, shall be cherished and nurtured, and made to grow and increase, till it comes unto perfection and he enters into " the inheritance of the saints in light." This is, as near as I can give it to you, the exact meaning and literal interpretation of the text, as I understand it.

But you may say to me, "In what sense is this meetness or fitness for eternal life the work of God the Father? Are we already made meet for heaven? How is this the Father's work?" Look at the text a moment, and I will answer you in three ways.

What is heaven? We read it is an *inheritance*. Who are fit for an inheritance? Sons. Who makes us sons? "Behold what manner of love *the Father* hath bestowed upon us, that we should be called the sons of God." A son is fitted for an inheritance. The moment the son is born he is fitted to be an heir. All that is wanted is that he shall grow up and be capable of possession. But he is fit for an inheritance at first. If he were not a son he could not inherit as an heir. Now, as soon as ever we become sons we are meet to inherit. There is in us an adaptation, a power and possibility for us to have an inheritance. This is the prerogative of the Father, to adopt us into his family, and to " beget us again unto a lively hope by the resurrection of Jesus Christ from the dead." And do you not see, that as adoption is really the meetness for inheritance, it is the Father who hath " made us meet to be partakers of the inheritance of the saints in light?"

Again, heaven is an inheritance; but whose inheritance is it? It is an inheritance of the *saints*. It is not an inheritance of sinners, but of saints—that is, of the holy ones—of those who have been made saints by being sanctified. Turn then, to the Epistle of Jude, and you will see at once who it is that sanctifies. You will observe the moment you fix your eye upon the passage that it is God the Father. In the first verse you read, " Jude, the servant of Jesus Christ, and brother of James, to them that are sanctified by God the Father." It is an inheritance for saints: and who are saints? The moment a man believes in Christ, he may know himself to have been truly set apart in the covenant decree; and he

8 SPECIAL THANKSGIVING TO THE FATHER

finds that consecration, if I may so speak, verified in his own experience, for he has now become "a new creature in Christ Jesus," separated from the rest of the world, and then it is manifest and made known that God has taken him to be his son for ever. The meetness which I must have, in order to enjoy the inheritance of the saints in light, is my becoming a son. God hath made me and all believers sons, therefore we are meet for the inheritance; so then that meetness has come from the Father. How meetly therefore doth the Father claim our gratitude, our adoration and our love!

You will however observe, it is not merely said that heaven is the inheritance of the saints, but that it is "the inheritance of the saints *in light.*" So the saints dwell in light—the light of knowledge, the light of purity, the light of joy, the light of love, pure ineffable love, the light of everything that is glorious and ennobling. There they dwell, and if I am to appear meet for that inheritance, what evidence must I have? I must have light shining into my own soul. But where can I get it? Do I not read that "every good gift and every perfect gift is from above, and cometh down"—yea verily, but from whom? From the Spirit? No—"from the Father of lights, with whom is no variableness, neither shadow of turning." The preparation to enter into the inheritance in light is light; and light comes from the Father of lights; therefore, my meetness, if I have light in myself, is the work of the Father, and I must give him praise. Do you see then, that as there are three words used here—"the *inheritance* of the *saints* in *light,*" so we have a threefold meetness? We are adopted and made sons. God hath sanctified us and set us apart. And then, again, he hath put light into our hearts. All this, I say, is the work of the Father, and in this sense, we are "meet to be partakers of the inheritance of the saints in light."

A few general observations here. Brethren, I am persuaded that if an angel from heaven were to come to-night and single out any one believer from the crowd here assembled, there is not one believer that is unfit to be taken to heaven. You may not be ready to be taken to heaven now; that is to say, if I foresaw that you were going to live, I would tell you you were unfit to die, in a certain sense. But were you to die now in your pew, if you believe in Christ, you are fit for heaven. You have a meetness even now which would take you there at once, without being committed to purgatory for a season. You are even now fit to be "partakers of the inheritance of the saints in light." You have but to gasp out your last breath and you shall be in heaven, and there shall not be one spirit in heaven more fit for heaven than you, nor one soul more adapted for the place than you are. You shall be just as fitted for its element as those who are nearest to the eternal throne.

Ah! this makes the heirs of glory think much of God the Father. When we reflect, my brethren, upon our state by nature, and how fit we are to be fire-brands in the flames of hell—yet to think that we are this night, at this very moment if Jehovah willed it, fit to sweep the golden harps with joyful fingers, that this head is fit this very night to wear the everlasting crown, that these loins are fit to be girded with that fair white robe throughout eternity, I say, this makes us think gratefully of God the Father; this makes us clap our hands with joy, and say, "Thanks be unto God the Father, who hath made us meet to be partakers of the inheritance of the saints in light." Do ye not remember the penitent thief? It was but a few minutes before that he had been cursing Christ. I doubt not that he had joined with the other, for it is said, "*They* that were crucified with him reviled him." Not one, but both; *they* did it. And then a gleam of supernatural glory lit up the face of Christ, and the thief saw and believed. And Jesus said unto him, "Verily I say unto thee, this day," though the sun is setting, "*this day* shalt thou be with me in Paradise." No long preparation required, no sweltering in purifying fires. And so shall it be with us. We may have been in Christ Jesus to our own knowledge but three weeks, or we may have been in him for ten years, or three-score years and ten—the date of our conversion makes no difference in our meetness for heaven, in a certain sense. True indeed the older we grow the more grace we have tasted, the riper we are becoming, and the fitter to be housed in heaven; but that is in another sense of the word,—the Spirit's meetness which he gives. But with regard to that meetness which the Father gives, I repeat, the blade of corn, the blade of gracious wheat that has just appeared above the surface of conviction, is as fit to be carried up to heaven as the full-grown corn in the ear. The sanctification wherewith we are sanctified by God the Father is not progressive, it is complete at once; we are now adapted for heaven, now fitted for it, and we shall be by-and-bye completely ready for it, and shall enter into the joy of our Lord.

Into this subject I might have entered more fully; but I have not time. I am sure I have left some knots untied, and you must untie them if you can yourselves; and let me recommend you to untie them on your knees—the mysteries of the kingdom of God are studied much the best when you are in prayer.

II. The second mercy is A MERCY THAT LOOKS BACK. We sometimes prefer the mercies that look forward, because they untold such a bright prospect.

"Sweet fields beyond the swelling flood."

But here is a mercy that looks backward; turns its back, as it were, on the heaven of our anticipation, and looks back on the gloomy past, and the dangers from which we have escaped. Let us read the account of it—"Who hath delivered us from the power of darkness, and hath translated us into the kingdom of his dear Son." This verse is an explanation of the preceding, as we shall have to show in a few minutes. But just now let us survey this mercy by itself. Ah! my brethren, what a description have we here of what manner of men we used to be. We *were* under "the power of darkness." Since I have been musing on this text, I have turned these words over and over in my mind—"the power of darkness!" It seems to me one of the most awful expressions that man ever attempted to expound. I think I could deliver a discourse from it, if God the Spirit helped me, which might make every bone in your body shake. "The power of darkness!" We all know that there is a *moral* darkness which exercises its awful spell over the mind of the sinner. Where God is unacknowledged the mind is void of judgment. Where God is unworshipped the heart of man becomes a ruin. The chambers of that dilapidated herrt are haunted by ghostly fears and degraded superstitions. The dark places of that reprobate mind are tenanted by vile lusts and noxious passions, like vermin and reptiles, from which in open daylight we turn with disgust. And even *natural* darkness is tremendous. In the solitary confinement which is practised in some of our penitentiaries the very worst results would be produced if the treatment were prolonged. If one of you were to be taken to-night and led into some dark cavern, and left there, I can imagine that for a moment, not knowing your fate, you might feel a child-like kind of interest about it;—there might be, perhaps, a laugh as you found yourselves in the dark; there might for the moment, from the novelty of the position, be some kind of curiosity excited. There might, perhaps, be a flush of silly joy. In a little time you might endeavour to compose yourself to sleep; possibly you might sleep; but if you should awake, and still find yourself down deep in the bowels of earth, where never a ray of sun or candle light could reach you; do you know the next feeling that would come over you? It would be a kind of idiotic thoughtlessness. You would find it impossible to control your desperate imagination. Your heart would say, "O God I am alone, alone, alone, in this dark place." How would you cast your eyeballs all around, and never catching a gleam of light, your mind would begin to fail. Your next stage would be one of increasing terror. You would fancy that you saw something, and then you would cry, "Ah! I would I could see something, were it foe or fiend!" You would feel the dark sides of your dungeon. You would begin to "scribble on the walls," like David before king Achish. Agitation would seize hold upon you, and if you were kept there much longer, delirium and death would be the consequence. We have heard of many who have been taken from the penitentiary to the lunatic asylum; and the lunacy is produced partly by the solitary confinement, and partly by the darkness in which they are placed. In a report lately written by the Chaplain of Newgate, there are some striking reflections upon the influence of darkness in a way of *discipline.* Its first effect is to shut the culprit up to his own reflections, and make him realize his true position in the iron grasp of the outraged law. Methinks the man that has defied his keepers, and come in there cursing and swearing, when he has found himself alone in darkness, where he cannot even hear the rattling of carriages along the streets, and can see no light whatever, is presently cowed; he gives in, he grows tame. "The power of darkness" literally is something awful. If I had time, I would enlarge upon this subject. We cannot properly describe what "the power of darkness" is, even in this world. The sinner is plunged into the darkness of his sins, and he sees nothing, he knows nothing. Let him remain there a little longer, and that joy of curiosity, that hectic joy which he now has in the path of sin, will die away, and there will come over him a spirit of slumber. Sin will make him drowsy, so that he will not hear the voice of the ministry, crying to him to escape for his life. Let him continue in it, and it will by-and-bye make him spiritually an idiot. He will become so set in sin, that common reason will be lost on him. All the arguments that a sensible man will receive, will be only wasted on him. Let him go on, and he will proceed from bad to worse, till he acquires the raving mania of a desperado in sin; and let death step in, and the darkness will have produced its full effect; he will come into the delirious madness of hell. Ah! it needs but the power of sin to make a man more truly hideous than human thought can realize, or language paint. Oh "the power of darkness!"

Now, my brethren, all of us were under this power once. It is but a few months—a few weeks with some of you—since you were under the power of darkness and of sin. Some of you had only got as far as the curiosity of it; others had got as far as the sleepiness of it; a good many of you had got as far as the apathy of it; and I do not know but some of you had got almost to the terror of it. You had so cursed and swore, so yelled ye out your blasphemies, that you seemed to be ripening for hell; but, praised and blessed be the name of the Father, he has "translated you from the power of darkness, into the kingdom of his dear Son."

Having thus explained this term, "the power of darkness," to show you what you were, let us take the next word, "and hath translated us." What a singular word this—"translated"—is. I dare say you think it means the process by which a word is interpreted, when the sense is retained, while the expression is rendered in another language. That is one meaning of the word "translation," but it is not the meaning here. The word is used by Josephus in this sense—the taking away of a people who have been dwelling in a certain country, and planting them in another place. This is called a translation. We sometimes hear of a bishop being translated or removed from one see to another. Now, if you want to have the idea explained, give me your attention while I bring out an amazing instance of a great translation. The children of Israel were in Egypt under taskmasters that oppressed them very sorely, and brought them into iron bondage. What did God do for these people? There were two millions of them. He did not temper the tyranny of the tyrant; he did not influence his mind, to give them a little more liberty; but he translated his people; he took the whole two millions bodily, with a high hand and outstretched arm, and led them through the wilderness, and translated them into the kingdom of Canaan; and there they were settled. What an achievement was that, when, with their flocks and their herds, and their little ones, the whole host of Israel went out of Egypt, crossed the Jordan, and came into Canaan! My dear brethren, the whole of it was not equal to the achievement of God's powerful grace, when he brings one poor sinner out of the region of sin into the kingdom of holiness and peace. It was easier for God to bring Israel out of Egypt, to split the Red Sea, to make a highway through the pathless wilderness, to drop manna from heaven, to send the whirlwind to drive out the kings; it was easier for Omnipotence to do all this, than to translate a man from the power of darkness into the kingdom of his dear Son. This is the grandest achievement of Omnipotence. The sustenance of the whole universe, I do believe, is even less than this—the changing of a bad heart, the subduing of an iron will. But thanks be unto the Father, he has done all that for you and for me. He has brought us out of darkness; he has translated us, taken up the old tree that has struck its roots never so deep—taken it up, blessed be God, roots and all, and planted it in a goodly soil. He had to cut the top off, it is true—the high branches of our pride; but the tree has grown better in the new soil than it ever did before. Who ever heard of moving so huge a plant as a man who has grown fifty years old in sin? Oh! what wonders hath our Father done for us! He has taken the wild leopard of the wood, tamed it into a lamb, and purged away its spots He has regenerated the poor Ethiop—oh, how black we were by nature—our blackness was more than skin deep; it went to the centre of our hearts; but, blessed be his name, he hath washed us white, and is still carrying on the divine operation, and he will yet completely deliver us from every taint of sin, and will finally bring us into the kingdom of his dear Son. Here, then, in the second mercy, we discern from what we were delivered, and how we were delivered—God the Father hath "translated" us.

But where are we now? Into what place is the believer brought, when he is brought out of the power of darkness? He is brought into the kingdom of God's dear Son. Into what other kingdom would the Christian desire to be brought? Brethren, a republic may sound very well in theory, but in spiritual matters, the last thing we want is a republic. We want a kingdom. I love to have Christ an absolute monarch in the heart. I do not want to have a doubt about it. I want to give up all my liberty to him, for I feel that I never shall be free till my self-control is all gone; that I shall never have my will truly free till it is bound in the golden fetters of his sweet love. We are brought into a kingdom—he is Lord and Sovereign, and he has made us "kings and priests unto our God," and we shall reign with him. The proof that we are in this kingdom must consist in our obedience to our King. Here, perhaps, we may raise many causes and questions, but surely we can say after all, though we have offended our King many times, yet our heart is loyal to him. "Oh, thou precious Jesus! we would obey thee, and yield submission to every one of thy laws; our sins are not wilful and beloved sins, but though we fall we can truly say, that we would be holy as thou art holy, our heart is true towards thy statutes; Lord, help us to run in the way of thy commandments."

So, you see, this mercy which God the Father hath given to us, this second of these present mercies, is, that he hath "translated us out of the power of darkness into the kingdom of his dear Son." This is the Father's work. Shall we not love God the Father from this day forth? Will we not give him thanks, and sing our hymns to him, and exalt and triumph in his great name?

III. Upon the third point, I shall be as brief as possible; it is to SHOW THE CONNECTION BETWEEN THE TWO VERSES.

When I get a passage of Scripture to meditate upon, I like, if I can, to see its drift; then I like to examine its various parts, and see if I can understand each separate clause; and then I want to go back again, and see what one clause has to do with another. I looked and looked again at this text, and wondered what connection there could be between the two verses. "Giving thanks unto God the Father, who hath made us meet to be partakers of the inheritance of the saints in light." Well, that is right enough; we can see how this is the work of God the Father, to make us meet to go to heaven. But has the next verse, the 13th, anything to do with our meetness?—"Who hath delivered us from the power of darkness, and hath translated us into the kingdom of his dear Son." Well, I looked it over, and I said I will read it in this way. I see the 12th verse tells me that the inheritance of heaven is the inheritance of light. Is heaven light? Then I can see my meetness for it as described in the 13th verse.--He hath delivered me from the power of darkness. Is not that the same thing? If I am delivered from the power of darkness, is not that being made meet to dwell in light? If I am now brought out of darkness into light, and am walking in the light, is not that the very meetness which is spoken of in the verse before? Then I read again. It says they are saints. Well, the saints are a people that obey the Son. Here is my meetness then in the 13th verse, where it says "He hath translated me from the power of darkness into the kingdom of his dear Son." So that I not only have the light, but the sonship too, for I am in "the kingdom of his dear Son." But how about the inheritance? Is there anything about that in the 13th verse? It is an inheritance; shall I find anything about a meetness for it there? Yes, I find that I am in the kingdom of his dear Son. How came Christ to have a kingdom? Why, by inheritance. Then it seems I am in his inheritance; and if I am in his inheritance here, then I am meet to be in it above, for I am in it already. I am even now part of it and partner of it, since I am in the kingdom which he inherits from his Father, and therefore there is the meetness.

I do not know whether I have put this plainly enough before you. If you will be kind enough to look at your Bible, I will just recapitulate. You see, heaven is a place of light; when we are brought out of darkness, that, of course, is the meetness for light. It is a place for sons; when we are brought into the kingdom of God's dear Son, we are of course made sons; so that there is the meetness for it. It is an inheritance; and when we are brought into the inherited kingdom of God's dear Son, we enjoy the inheritance now, and consequently are fitted to enjoy it for ever.

Having thus shown the connection between these verses, I propose now to close with a few general observations. I like so to expound the Scripture, that we can draw some practical inferences from it. Of course the first inference is this: let us from this night forward never omit God the Father in our praises. I think I have said this already six times over in the sermon. Why I am repeating it so often, is that we may never forget it. Martin Luther said he preached upon justification by faith every day in the week, and then the people would not understand. There are some truths, I believe, that need to be said over and over again, either because our silly hearts will not receive, or our treacherous memories will not hold them. Sing, I beseech you, habitually, the praises of the Father in heaven, as you do the praises of the Son hanging upon the cross. Love as truly

God, the ever-living God, as you love Jesus the God-man, the Saviour who once died for you. That is the great inference.

Yet another inference arises. Brothers and sisters, are you conscious to-night that you are not now what you once were? Are you sure that the power of darkness does not now rest upon you, that you love divine knowledge, that you are panting after heavenly joys? Are you sure that you have been "translated into the kingdom of God's dear Son?" Then never be troubled about thoughts of death, because. come death whenever it may, you are meet to be a "partaker of the inheritance of the saints in light." Let no thought distress you about death's coming to you at an unseasonable hour. Should it come to-morrow, should it come now, if your faith is fixed on nothing less than Jesu's blood and righteousness, you shall see the face of God with acceptance. I have that consciousness in my soul, by the witness of the Holy Spirit, of my adoption into the family of God, that I feel that though I should never preach again, but should lay down my body and my charge together, ere I should reach my home, and rest in my bed, "I know that my Redeemer liveth," and more, that I should be a "partaker of the inheritance of the saints in light." It is not always that one feels that; but I would have you never rest satisfied till you do, till you know your meetness, till you are conscious of it; until, moreover. you are panting to be gone, because you feel that you have powers which never can be satisfied short of heaven—powers which heaven only can employ.

One more reflection lingers behind. There are some of you here that cannot be thought by the utmost charity of judgment, to be "meet for the inheritance of the saints in light." Ah! if a wicked man should go to heaven without being converted, heaven would be no heaven to him. Heaven is not adapted for sinners; it is not a place for them. If you were to take a Hottentot who has long dwelt at the equator up to where the Esquimaux are dwelling. and tell him that you would show him the aurora, and all the glories of the North Pole, the poor wretch could not appreciate them; he would say, "It is not the element for me; it is not the place where I could rest happy!" And if you were to take, on the other hand, some dwarfish dweller in the north, down to the region where trees grow to a stupendous height, and where the spices give their balmy odours to the gale, and bid him live there under the torrid zone, he could enjoy nothing; he would say, "This is not the place for me. because it is not adapted to my nature." Or if you were to take the vulture, that has never fed on anything but carrion, and put it into the noblest dwelling you could make for it, and feed it with the daintiest meals, it would not be happy because it is not food that is adapted for it. And you, sinner, you are nothing but a carrion vulture; nothing makes you happy but sin; you do not want too much psalm singing, do you? Sunday is a dull day to you; you like to get it over, you do not care about your Bible; you would as soon there should be no Bible at all. You find that going to a meeting-house or a church is very dull-work indeed. Oh then you will not be troubled with that in eternity; do not agitate yourself. If you love not God, and die as you are, you shall go to your own company, you shall go to your jolly mates, you shall go to your good fellows, those who have been your mates on earth shall be your mates for ever; but you shall go to the Prince of those good fellows, unless you repent and be converted. Where God is you cannot come. It is not an element suited to you. As well place a bird at the bottom of the sea, or a fish in the air, as place an ungodly sinner in heaven. What is to be done then? You must have a new nature. I pray God to give it to you. Rremember if now you feel your need of a Saviour, that is the beginning of the new nature. "Believe on the Lord Jesus Christ;" cast yourselves simply on him, trust in nothing but his blood, and then the new nature shall be expanded, and you shall be made meet by the Holy Spirit's operations to be a "partaker of the inheritance of the saints in light." There is many a man who has come into this house of prayer, many a man is now present, who has come in here a rollicking fellow, fearing neither God nor devil. Many a man has come from the ale house up to this place. If he had died then. where would his soul have been? But the Lord that very night met him. There are trophies of that grace present here to-night. You can say, "Thanks be to the Father, who hath brought us out of the power of darkness, and translated us into the kingdom of his dear Son." And if God has done that for some. why cannot he do it for others? Why need you despair, O poor sinner? If thou art here to-night, the worst sinner out of hell, remember, the gate of mercy stands wide open, and Jesus bids thee come. Conscious of thy guilt, flee, flee to him. Look to his cross. and thou shalt find pardon in his veins, and life in his death.

2. Jesus the Example of Holy Praise

"I will declare thy name unto my brethren: in the midst of the congregation will I praise thee. Ye that fear the Lord, praise him; all ye the seed of Jacob, glorify him; and fear him, all ye the seed of Israel."—Psalm xxii. 22, 23.

WE greatly esteem the dying words of good men, but what must be the value of their departing thoughts! If we could pass beyond the gate of speech, and see the secret things which are transacted in the silent chambers of their souls in the moment of departure, we might greatly value the revelation, for there are thoughts which the tongue could not and must not utter, and there are deep searchings of heart which are not to be expressed by syllables and sentences. If, by some means, we could read the inmost death-thoughts of holy men, we might be privileged indeed. Now, in the Psalm before us, and in the words of our text, we have the last thoughts of our Lord and Master, and they beautifully illustrate the fact that he was governed by one ruling passion: that ruling passion most strong in death, was the glory of God. When but a child, he said, "Wist ye not that I must be about my Father's business?" Throughout his work-life he could say, "The zeal of thine house hath eaten me up;" "It is my meat and my drink to do the will of him that sent me;" and now, at last, as he expires, with his hands and his feet nailed, and his body and soul in extreme anguish, the one thought is, that God may be glorified. In that last happy interval, before he actually gave up his soul into his Father's hands, his thoughts rushed forward and found a blessed place of rest in the prospect that, as the result of his death, all the kindreds of the nations would worship before the Lord, and that by a chosen seed the Most High should be honoured. O for the same concentration of all our powers upon one thing, and that one thing, the glory of God! Would God that we could say with one of old, "This one thing I do," and that this one thing might be the chief end of our being, the glorifying of our Creator, our Redeemer, the liege Lord of our hearts.

My object, this morning, is to excite in you the spirit of adoring gratitude. I thought that as last Sabbath we spoke of Christ as the example of protracted prayer, it might seem seasonable at the end of a month of so much mercy to exhibit him to you as the example of grateful praise, and to ask you as a great congregation to follow him as your leader in the delightful exercise of magnifying the name of Jehovah.

> " Far away be gloom and sadness ;
> Spirits with seraphic fire,
> Tongues with hymns, and hearts with gladness,
> Higher sound the chords and higher."

I shall ask your attention, in considering these verses, first, to *our Lord's example* : " I will declare thy name unto my brethren : in the midst of the congregation will I praise thee ;" and, secondly, I shall invite you to observe *our Lord's exhortation ;* " Ye that fear the Lord, praise him ; all ye the seed of Jacob, glorify him ; and fear him, all ye the seed of Israel."

I. We begin with OUR LORD'S EXAMPLE.

The praise which our Jesus as our exemplar renders unto the eternal Father is twofold. First, *the praise of declaration,* "I will *declare* thy name unto my brethren;" and, secondly, *the more direct and immediate thanksgiving,* " In the midst of the congregation will I praise thee."

1. The first form of the praise which our blessed Mediator renders unto the eternal Father, is that of *declaring God's name.* This, my dear friends, you know he did *in his teaching.* Something of God had been revealed to men aforetime; God had spoken to Noah and Abraham, and Isaac and Jacob, and especially to his servant Moses; he had been pleased to discover himself in divers types and ceremonies and ordinances. He was known as Elohim, Shaddai, and Jehovah, but never until Christ came did men begin to say, " Our Father which art in heaven." This was the loving word by which the Wellbeloved declared his Father's name unto his brethren. The sterner attributes of God had been discovered amidst the thunders of Sinai, the waves of the Red Sea, the smoke of Sodom, and the fury of the deluge ; the sublimities of the Most High had been seen, and wondered at by the prophets who spoke as they were moved by the Holy Ghost; but the full radiance of a Father's love was never seen till it was beheld beaming through the Saviour's face. " He that hath seen me," said Christ, "hath seen the Father ; " but until they had seen him they had not seen God as the Father. " No man can come unto the Father," saith Jesus, " except by me ;" and as no man can come affectionately in the outgoings of his heart, or fiducially in the motions of his faith, so neither can any man come to God in the enlightenment of understanding except by Christ the Son. He who understands Christianity has a far better idea of God than he who only comprehends Judaism. Read the Old Testament through, and you shall value every sentence, and prize it above fine gold, but still you shall feel unrest and dissatisfaction, for the vision is veiled, and the light is dim; turn then to the New Testament, and you discern that in Jesus of Nazareth dwelleth all the fulness of the Godhead bodily, and the noontide of knowledge is around you, the vision is open and distinct. Jesus is the express image of his Father's person, and seeing him you have seen God manifest in the flesh. This sight of God you will assuredly obtain if you are one of the brethren to whom, through the Spirit, Jesus Christ in his teaching declares the name of the Father.

Our Lord, however, declared the Father more perhaps *by his acts* than by his words, for the life of Christ is a discovery of all the attributes of God in action. If you want to know the gentleness of God, you perceive Jesus receiving sinners and eating with them. If you would know his condescension, behold the loving Redeemer taking little children into his arms and blessing them. If you would know whether God is just, hear the words of a Saviour as he denounces sin, and observe his own life, for he is holy, harmless, undefiled, and separate from sinners. Would you know the mercy of God as well as his justice? then see it manifested in the ten thousand miracles of the Saviour's hands, and in the constant sympathy of the Redeemer's heart. I cannot stay to bring out all the incidents in the Redeemer's life, nor even to give you a brief sketch of it, but suffice it to say, that the life of Christ is a perpetual unrolling of the great mystery of the divine attributes, and you may rest assured that what Jesus is, that the Father is. You need not start back from the Father, as though he were something strange and unrevealed, for you have seen the Father if you have seen Christ; and if you have studied well and drunk deep into the spirit of the history of the Man of sorrows, you understand, as well as you need to do, the character of God over all, blessed for ever.

Our Lord made the grandest declaration of the Godhead *in his death.*

> " Here his whole name appears complete,
> Nor wit can guess, nor reason trace,
> Which of the letters best is writ—
> The power, the wisdom, or the grace."

There at Calvary, where he suffered the just for the unjust to bring us to God, we see the Godhead resplendent in noonday majesty, albeit that to the natural eye it seems to be eclipsed in midnight gloom. Would you see stern justice such as the Judge of all the earth perpetually exhibits (for shall not he do right)? Would you see the justice that will not spare the guilty, which smites at sin with determined enmity and will not endure it? Then behold the hands and feet, and side of the Redeemer, welling up with crimson blood! Behold his heart broken as with an iron rod, dashed to shivers as though it were a potter's vessel! Hearken to his cries; mark the lines of grief that mar his face; behold the turmoil, the confusion, the whirlwinds of anguish which seethe like a boiling caldron within the soul of the Redeemer! Here is the vengeance of God revealed to men, so that they may see it and not die, may behold it and weep, but not with the tears of despair. At the same time, if you would see the grace of God, where shall you discover it as you will in the death of Jesus? God's bounty gleams in the light, flashes in the rain and sparkles in the dew; it blossoms in the flowers that bestud the meadows, and it ripens in the golden sheaves of autumn. All God's works are full of goodness and truth; even on the sea itself are the steps of the beneficent Creator; but all this does not meet the case of guilty, condemned man, and, therefore, to the eye of him who has learned to weep for sin, nature does not reveal the goodness of God in any such a light as that which gleams from the cross. Best of all is God seen as he that spared not his own Son, but freely delivered him up for us all. " Herein is love, not that we loved God, but that he loved us," " For God commendeth his love toward us, in that while we were yet sinners, Christ died for us." Your thoughtful minds will readily discover every one of the great qualities of Deity in our dying Lord. You have only to linger long enough amidst the wondrous scenes of Gethsemane, and Gabbatha, and Golgotha, to observe how power and wisdom, grace and vengeance, strangely join—

> " Piercing his Son with sharpest smart,
>   To make the purchased blessing mine."

Beloved, in the midst of the brethren, a dying Saviour declares the name of the Lord, and thus magnifies the Lord as no other can. None of the harps of angels, nor the fiery, flaming, sonnets of cherubs can glorify God as did the wounds and pangs of the great Substitute when he died to make his Father's grace and justice known.

Our Lord continued to declare God's name among his brethren when *he rose from the dead.* He did so literally. Amongst the very first words he said were, " Go to my brethren;" and his message was, " I ascend unto my Father, and your Father; and to my God, and your God." His life on earth after his resurrection was but brief, but it was very rich and instructive, and in itself a showing forth of divine faithfulness. He further revealed the faithfulness and glory of God, when he ascended on high, leading captivity captive. It must have been an august day when the Son of God actually passed the pearly gates to remain within the walls of heaven enthroned until his second advent ! How must the spirits of just men made perfect have risen from their seats of bliss to gaze on him ! They had not seen a risen one before. Two had passed into heaven without death, but none had entered into glory as risen from the dead. He was the first instance of immortal resurrection, " the first-fruits of them that slept." How angels adored him ! How holy beings wondered at him while

> " The God shone gracious through the man,
>   And shed sweet glories on them all !"

Celestial spirits saw the Lord that day as they had never seen before ! They had worshipped God, but the excessive splendour of absolute Deity had forbidden the sacred familiarity with which they hailed the Lord in flesh arrayed. They were never so near Jehovah before, for in Christ the Godhead veiled its killing splendours, and wore the aspect of a fatherhood and brotherhood most near and dear. Enough was seen of glory, as much as finite beings could bear, but still the whole was so sweetly shrouded in humanity, that God was declared in a new and more delightful manner, such as made heaven ring with new-born joy.

What if I say that methinks a part of the occupation of Christ *in heaven* is to declare to perfect spirits what he suffered, how God sustained him, to reveal to them the covenant, and all its solemn bonds, how the

Lord ordained it, how he made it firm by suretyships, and based it upon eternal settlements, so that everlasting mercy might flow from it. What if it be not true that there is no preaching in heaven! What if Christ be the preacher there, speaking as never man spake, and for ever instructing his saints that they may make known unto principalities and powers yet more fully the manifold wisdom of God as revealed both in him and in them—in them the members, and in him the Head! Methinks, if it be so, it is a sweet fulfilment of this dying vow of our blessed Master, "I will declare thy name unto my brethren."

But, brethren, it is certain that at this hour our Lord Jesus Christ continues to fulfil the vow by *the spreading of his gospel on earth.* Do not tell me that *the gospel* does declare God, but that Jesus does not so. I would remind you that the gospel does not declare God apart from the the presence of Jesus Christ with the gospel. "Lo, I am with you alway, even to the end of the world," is the gospel's true life and power. Take Christ's presence away, and all the doctrines, and the precepts, and the invitations of the gospel would not declare God to this blind-eyed generation, this hard-hearted multitude, but where Jesus is by his Spirit, there by the word the Father is declared. And, my brethren, this great process will go on. All through the present dispensation, Christ will declare God to the sons of men, especially to the elect sons of men, to his own brethren. Then shall come the latter days of which we know so little, but of which we hope so much. Then, in that august period there will be a declaration, no doubt, of God in noonday light, for it shall be said, " The tabernacle of God is with men, and he shall dwell among them." Of that age of light Jesus shall be the sun. The great revealer of Deity shall still be the Son of Mary, the Man of Nazareth, the Wonderful, the Counsellor, the Mighty God, the everlasting Father, the Prince of Peace; we shall each one of us tell abroad the savour of his name till he shall come, and then we shall have no need to say one to another, " Know the Lord," for all shall know him, from the least to the greatest; and know the Lord for this reason, because they know Christ, and have seen Jehovah in the person of Jesus Christ his Son.

I cannot leave this passage without bidding you treasure up that precious word of our Master, "I will declare thy name unto *my brethren.*"

> " Our next of kin, our brother now,
> Is he to whom the angels bow;
> They join with us to praise his name,
> But we the nearest interest claim."

" Forasmuch then as the children are partakers of flesh and blood, he also himself likewise took part of the same." " For both he that sanctifieth and they who are sanctified are all of one : for which cause he is not ashamed to call them brethren." The Saviour's brethren are to know God in Christ; you who are one with Jesus, you who have been adopted into the same family, have been regenerated and quickened with his life, you who are joined together by an indissoluble union, you are to see the Lord. I said an indissoluble union, for a wife may be divorced, but there is no divorce of brethren. I never heard of any law, human or divine, that could ever unbrother a man; that cannot be done; if a man be my brother, he is and shall be my brother when heaven and earth shall pass away. Am I Jesus' brother? Then I am joint heir with him; I share in all he has, and all that God bestows upon him; his Father is my Father; his God is my God. Feast, my brethren, on this dainty meat, and go your way in the strength of it to bear the trials of earth with more than patience.

The example of our Lord, under this first head, I must hint at and leave. It is this: if the Lord Jesus Christ declares God, especially to his own brethren, be it your business and mine, in order to praise Jehovah, to tell out what we know of the excellence and surpassing glories of our God; and especially let us do it to our kinsfolk, our household, our neighbours, and, since all men are in a sense our brethren, let us speak of Jesus wherever our lot is cast. My brethren and sisters, I wish we talked more of our God.

> "But ah! how faint our praises rise!
> Sure 'tis the wonder of the skies,
> That we, who share his richest love,
> So cold and unconcern'd should prove."

How many times this week have you praised the dear Redeemer to your friends? Have you done it once? I do it often officially; but I wish I did it more often, spontaneously and personally, to those with whom I may commune by the way. You have doubtless murmured this week, or spoken against your neighbours, or spread abroad some small amount of scandal, or, it may be, you have talked frothily and with levity. It is even possible that impurity has been in your speech; even a Christian's language is not always so pure as it should be. Oh, if we saved our breath to praise God with, how much wiser! If our mouth were filled with the Lord's praise and with his honour all the day, how much holier! If we would but speak of what Jesus has done for us, what good we might accomplish! Why, every man speaks of what he loves! Men can hardly hold their tongues about their inventions and their delights. Speak well, O ye faithful, of the Lord's name. I pray you, be not dumb concerning one who deserves so well of you; but make this the resolve of this Sabbath morning, "I will declare thy name unto my brethren."

2. Our Master's second form of *praise* in the text is *of a more direct kind*—"In the midst of the congregation will I praise thee." Is it a piece of imagination, or does the text really mean this, that the Lord Jesus Christ, as man, adores and worships the eternal God in heaven,

and is, in fact, the great Leader of the devotions of the skies? Shall I err if I say that they all bow when he as Priest adores the Lord, and all lift up the voice at the lifting up of his sacred psalmody? Is he the chief Musician of the sky, the Master of the sacred choir? Does he beat time for all the hallelujahs of the universe? I think so. I think he means that in these words: "In the midst of the congregation will I praise thee." As God, he is praised for ever: far above all worshipping, he is himself for ever worshipped; but as Man, the Head of redeemed humanity, the everliving Priest of the Most High God, I believe that he praises Jehovah in heaven. Surely it is the office of the Head to speak and to represent the holy joys and devout aspirations of the whole body which he represents.

In the midst of the congregations of earth, too, is not Jesus Christ the sweetest of all singers? I like to think that when we pray on earth our prayers are not alone, but our great High Priest is there to offer our petitions with his own. When we sing on earth it is the same. Is not Jesus Christ in the midst of the congregation, gathering up all the notes which come from sincere lips, to put them into the golden censer, and to make them rise as precious incense before the throne of the infinite majesty? So that *he* is the great singer, rather than we. He is the chief player on our stringed instruments, the great master of true music. The worship of earth comes up to God through him, and he, *he* is the accepted channel of all the praise of all the redeemed universe.

I am anticipating the day—I hope we are all longing for it—when the dead shall rise and the sea and land shall give up the treasured bodies of the saints, and glorified spirits shall descend to enliven their renovated frames, and we who are alive and remain shall be changed and made immortal, and the King himself shall be revealed. Then shall be trodden under our feet all the ashes of our enemies; Satan, bound, shall be held beneath the foot of Michael, the great archangel, and victory shall be on the side of truth and righteousness. What a "Hallelujah" that will be which shall peal from land and sea and from islands of the far-off main—"Hallelujah! Hallelujah! Hallelujah! the Lord God omnipotent reigneth!" Who will lead that song? Who shall be the first to praise God in that day of triumph? Who first shall wave the palm of victory? Who but he who was first in the fight and first in the victory, he who trod the wine-press alone and stained his garments with the blood of his enemies, he that cometh from Edom, with dyed garments from Bozrah—surely he it is who in the midst of the exulting host, once militant and then triumphant, shall magnify and adore Jehovah's name for ever and for ever. Hath he not himself said it, "My praise shall be of thee in the great congregation"?

What means that expression so hard to be understood, "Then cometh the end, when he shall have delivered up the kingdom to God, even the

Father"? What means that dark saying, "And when all things shall be subdued unto him, then shall the Son also himself be subject unto him that put all things under him, that God may be all in all"? Whatever it may mean, it seems to teach us the mediatorial crown and government are temporary, and intended only to last until all rule, and all authority and power, are put down by Jesus, and the rule of God shall be universally acknowledged. Jesus cannot renounce his Godhead, but his mediatorial sovereignty will be yielded up to him from whom it came, and that last solemn act, in which he shall hand back to his Father the all-subduing sceptre, will be a praising of God to a most wonderful extent beyond human conception. We wait and watch for it, and we shall behold it in the time appointed.

Beloved friends, we have in this second part also an example: let *us* endeavour to praise our God in a direct manner. We ought to spend at least a little time every day in adoring contemplation. Our private devotions are scarcely complete if they consist altogether of prayer. Should there not be praise? If possible, during each day, sing a hymn. Perhaps you are not in a position to sing it aloud, very loud, at any rate, but I would hum it over, if I were you. Many of you working men find time enough to sing a silly song, why cannot you find space for the praise of God? Every day let us praise him, when the eyelids of the morning first are opened, and when the curtains of the night are drawn, ay, and at midnight, if we wake at that solemn hour, let the heart put fire to the sacred incense and present it unto the Lord that liveth for ever and ever. In the midst of the congregation also, whenever we come up to God's house, let us take care that our praise is not merely lip language, but that of the heart. Let us all sing, and so sing that God himself shall hear. We need more than the sweet sounds which die upon mortal ears, we want the deep melodies which spring from the heart, and which enter into the ears of the immortal God. Imitate Jesus, then, in this twofold praise, the declaring of God, and the giving of direct praise to him.

II. My time almost fails me, while I have need of much of it, for now I come to the second head, OUR LORD'S EXHORTATION.

Follow me earnestly, my dear brethren and sisters, and then follow me practically also. The exhortations of the second verse are given to those who fear God, who have respect to him, who tremble to offend him, who carry with them the consciousness of his presence into their daily life, who act towards him as obedient children towards a father. The exhortation is further addressed to the seed of Jacob, to those in covenant with God, to those who have despised the pottage and chosen the birthright, to those who, if they have had to sleep with a stone for their pillow, have, nevertheless, seen heaven opened, and enjoyed a revelation of God, to those who know what prevalence in prayer means, to those who, in all their trouble, have yet found that all these things are not against them, but work their everlasting good, for Jesus is yet alive, and they shall see him ere they die. It is, moreover, directed to the seed of Israel, to those who once were in Egypt, in spiritual bondage, who have been brought out of slavery, who are being guided through the wilderness, fed with heaven's manna, and made to drink of the living Rock, to those who worship the one God and him only, and put away their idols and desire to be found always obedient to the Master's will. Now, to them it is said, first, " Praise him." Praise him *vocally*. I wish that in every congregation every child of God would take pains to praise God with his mouth as well as with his heart. Do you know, I have noticed one thing—I have jotted this down in the diary of my recollection—that you always sing best when you are most spiritual. Last Monday night the singing was very much better than it was on Sabbath evening. You kept better time and better tune, not because the tune was any easier, but because you had come up to worship God with more solemnity than usual, and therefore there was no slovenly singing such as pains my ear and heart sometimes. Why, some of you care so little to give the Lord your best music, that you fall half a note behind the rest, others of you are singing quite a false note, and a few make no sound of any kind. I hate to enter a place of worship where half-a-dozen sing to the praise and glory of themselves, and the rest stand and listen. I like that good old plan of everybody singing, singing his best, singing carefully and heartily. If you cannot sing artistically, never mind, you will be right enough if you sing from the heart, and pay attention to it, and do not drawl out like a musical machine that has been set agoing, and therefore runs on mechanically. With a little care the heart brings the art, and the heart desiring to praise will by-and-by train the voice to time and tune. I would have our service of song to be of the best. I care not for the fineries of music, and the prettinesses of chants and anthems. As for instrumental music, I fear that it often destroys the singing of the congregation, and detracts from the spirituality and simplicity of worship. If I could crowd a house twenty times as big as this by the fine music which some churches delight in, God forbid I should touch it; but let us have the best and most orderly harmony we can make—let the saints come with their hearts in the best humour, and their voices in the best tune, and let them take care that there be no slovenliness and discord in the public worship of the Most High.

Take care to praise God also *mentally*. The grandest praise that floats up to the throne is that which arises from silent contemplation and reverent thought. Sit down and think of the greatness of God, his love, his power, his faithfulness, his sovereignty, and as your mind bows prostrate before his majesty, you will have praised him, though not a sound shall have come from you.

Praise God also by your *actions*, your sacrifice to him of your property, your offering to him week by week of your substance. This is true praise, and far less likely to be hypocritical than the mere thanksgiving of words, " Ye that fear the Lord, praise him."

The texts adds, "*Glorify him*, ye seed of Jacob "—another form of the same thing. Glorify God, that is, let others know of his glory. Let them know of it from what you say, but specially let them know of it from what you *are*. Glorify God in your business, in your recreations, in your shops and in your households. In whatsoever ye eat and drink, glorify the Lord. In the commonest actions of life wear the vestments of your sacred calling, and act as a royal priesthood serving the Most High. Glorify your Creator and Redeemer. Glorify him by endeavouring to spread abroad the gospel which glorifies him. Magnify Christ by explaining to men how by believing they shall find peace in him. Glorify God by yourself boldly relying on his word, in the teeth of afflicting providence, and over the head of all suspicions and mistrust. Nothing can glorify God more than an Abrahamic faith which staggers not at the promise through unbelief. O ye wrestling seed of Jacob, see to it that ye fall not off in the matter of glorifying your God.

Lastly, the text says, " *Fear him*," as if this were one of the highest methods of praise. Walk in his sight; constantly keep the Lord before you; let him be at your right hand. Sin not, for in so doing you dishonour him. Suffer rather than sin. Choose the burning fiery furnace rather than bow down before the golden image. Be willing to be yourself despised, sooner than God should be despised. Be content to bear the cross, rather than Jesus should be crucified afresh. Be put to shame, sooner than Jesus should be put to shame. Thus you will truly praise and magnify the name of the Most High.

I must close by a few remarks which are meant to assist you to carry out the spirit and teaching of this sermon. Beloved brethren and sisters, this morning I felt, before I came to this place, very much in the spirit of adoring gratitude. I cannot communicate that to you, but the Spirit of God can; and the thoughts that helped me to praise God were something like these—let me give them to you as applied to yourselves—glorify and praise God, for he has saved you, *has* saved you, saved you from hell, saved you for heaven. Oh, how much is comprehended in the fact that you are saved! Think of the election which ordained you to salvation, the covenant which secured salvation to you; think of the incarnation by which God came to you, and the precious blood by which you now have been made nigh to God. Hurry not over those thoughts though I must shorten my words. Linger at each one of these sacred fountains and drink, and when you have seen what salvation involves in the past, think of what it means in the future. You shall be preserved to the end; you shall be educated in the school of grace; you shall be admitted into the home of the blessed in the land of the hereafter. You shall have a resurrection most glorious, and an immortality most illustrious. When days and years are passed, a crown shall adorn your brow, a harp of joy shall fill your hand. All this is yours, believer; and will you not praise him? Make any one of them stand right out, as real to you personally, and methinks you will say, "Should I refuse to sing, sure the very stones would speak." Your God has done more than this for you. You are not barely saved, like a drowning man just dragged to the bank; you have had more given you than you ever lost. You have been a gainer by Adam's fall. You might almost say, as one of the fathers did, *O beata culpa*, "O happy fault," which put me into the position to be so richly endowed as now I am! Had you stood in Adam, you had never been able to call Jesus "Brother," for there had been no need for him to become incarnate; you had never been washed in the precious blood, for then it had no need to be shed. Jesus has restored that to you which he took not away. He has not merely lifted you from the dunghill to set you among men, but to set you among princes, even the princes of his people. Think of the bright roll of promises, of the rich treasure of covenant provision, of all that you have already had and all that Christ has guaranteed to you of honour, and glory, and immortality, and will you not in the midst of the congregation praise the Lord? Brethren and sisters, some of us have had especial cause for praising God, in the fact that we have seen many saved during the last three weeks, and amongst them those dear to us. Mothers, can you hear the fact without joy? your children saved! Brothers, your sisters saved! Fathers, your sons and daughters saved! How many has God brought in during the last few weeks? And you Sunday-school teachers, who have been the instruments of this, you conductors of our classes, who have been honoured of God to be spiritual parents, you elders and deacons, who have helped us so nobly, and who have now to share the joy of the pastor's heart in these conversions, will you not bless God? "Not unto us, not unto us, but unto thy name be praise." But oh! we cannot be silent; not one tongue shall silent be; we will all magnify and bless the Most High. Brethren and sisters, if these do not suffice to make us praise him, I would say, think of God's own glorious self! Think of Father, Son, and Spirit, and what the triune Jehovah is in his own person and attributes, and if you do not praise him, oh, how far must you have backslidden! Remember the host who now adore him. When we bless him, we stand not alone : angels and archangels are at our right hand, cherubim and seraphim are in the selfsame choir. The notes of redeemed men go not up alone, they are united to, and swollen by, the unceasing flood of praise which flows from the hierarchy of angels. Think, beloved, of how you will praise him soon! how, ere many days and weeks are passed, many of us will be with the glorious throng. This last week three of our number have been translated to the skies: more links to heaven, fewer bonds to earth. They have gone before us, we had almost said, "Would God it were our lot instead of theirs;" they have seen now what eye hath not seen, and heard what ear hath never heard, and their spirits have drunk in what they could not else have conceived. We shall soon be there! Meanwhile, let each one of us sing—

> "I would begin the music here,
>   And so my soul should rise:
> Oh! for some heavenly notes to bear
>   My passions to the skies!
>
> There ye that love my Saviour sit,
>   There I would fain have place
> Among your thrones, or at your feet,
>   So I might see *his* face."

3. Laus Deo

"For of him, and through him, and to him, are all things : to whom be glory for ever. Amen."—Romans xi. 36.

MY text consists almost entirely of monosyllables, but it contains the loftiest of sublimities. Such a tremendous weight of meaning is concentrated here, that an archangel's eloquence would fail to convey its teaching in all its glory to any finite minds, even if seraphs were his hearers. I will affirm that there is no man living who can preach from my text a sermon worthy of it; nay, that among all the sacred orators and the eloquent pleaders for God, there never did live and never will live, a man capable of reaching the height of the great argument contained in these few simple words. I utterly despair of success, and will not therefore make an attempt to work out the infinite glory of this sentence. Our great God alone can expound this verse, for he only knows himself, and he only can worthily set forth his own perfections. Yet I am comforted by this reflection that, may be, in answer to our prayers, God himself may preach from this text this morning in our hearts; if not through the words of the speaker, yet by that still small voice to which the believer's ear is so well accustomed. If thus he shall condescend to favour us, our hearts shall be lifted up in his ways.

There are two things before us, the one worthy of our observation, and the second of our imitation. You have in the text first of all, doctrine, and then devotion. The doctrine is high doctrine—"Of him, and through him, and to him, are all things." The devotion is lofty devotion—"To whom be glory for ever. Amen."

I. Let us consider THE DOCTRINE. It is laid down by the apostle Paul, as a general principle, that all things come of God: they are *of* him as their *source;* they are *through* him as their *means;* they are *to* him as their *end.* They are *of* him in the *plan, through* him in the *working,* and *to* him in the *glory* which they produce. Taking this general principle, you will find it apply to all things, and be it ours to mark those in which it is most manifestly the case. May the Lord, by his Holy Spirit, open his treasures to us at this moment, that we may be enriched in spiritual knowledge and understanding.

Meditate, dear friends, upon *the whole range of God's works in creation and providence*. There was a period when God dwelt alone and creatures were not. In that time before all time, when there was no day but "The Ancient of Days," when matter and created mind were alike unborn, and even space was not, God, the great I Am, was as perfect, glorious, and blessed as he is now. There was no sun, and yet Jehovah dwelt in light ineffable; there was no earth, and yet his throne stood fast and firm; there were no heavens, and yet his glory was unbounded. God inhabited eternity in the infinite majesty and happiness of his self-contained greatness. If the Lord, thus abiding in awful solitude, should choose to create anything, the first thought and idea must come of him, for there was no other to think or suggest. All things must be *of him* in design. With whom can he take counsel? Who shall instruct him? There existed not another to come into the council-chamber, even if such an assistance could be supposable with the Most High. In the beginning of his way before his works of old, eternal wisdom brought forth from its own mind the perfect plan of future creations, and every line and mark therein must clearly have been of the Lord alone. He ordained the pathway of every planet, and the abode of every fixed star. He poured forth the sweet influences of the Pleiades, and girt Orion with his bands. He appointed the bounds of the sea, and settled the course of the winds. As to the earth, the Lord alone planned its foundations, and stretched his line upon it. He formed in his own mind the mould of all his creatures and found for them a dwelling and a service. He appointed the degree of strength with which he would endow each creature, settled its months of life, its hour of death, its coming and its going. Divine wisdom mapped this earth, its flowing rivers and foaming seas, the towering mountains, and the laughing valleys. The divine Architect fixed the gates of the morning and the doors of the shadow of death. Nothing could have been suggested by any other, for there was no other to suggest. It was in his power to have made a universe very different from this, if he had so pleased; and that he has made it what it is, must have been merely because in his wisdom and prudence he saw fit to do so. There cannot be any reason why he should not have created a world from which sin should have been for ever excluded; and that he suffered sin to enter into his creation must again be ascribed to his own infinite sovereignty. Had he not well known that he would be master over sin, and out of evil evolve the noblest display of his own glory, he had not permitted it to enter into the world: but, in sketching the whole history of the universe which he was about to create, he permitted even that black spot to defile his work, because he foreknew what songs of everlasting triumph would rise to himself when, in streams of his own blood, incarnate Deity should wash out the stain. It cannot be doubted that whatever may be the whole drama of history in creation and providence, there is a high and mysterious sense in which it is all of God. The sin is not God's, but the temporary permission of its existence formed part of the foreknown scheme, and to our faith the intervention of moral evil, and the purity of the divine character, do neither of them diminish the force of our belief that the whole scope of history is *of God* in the fullest sense.

When the plan was all laid down, and the Almighty had ordered his purpose, this was not enough: mere arrangement would not create. "*Through* him," as well as "*of* him," must all things be. There was no raw material ready to the Creator's hand; he must create the universe out of nothing. He calleth not for aid—he needs it not, and besides, there is none to help him. There is no rough matter which he may fashion between his palms and launch forth as stars. He did not need a mine of unquarried matter which he might melt and purify in the furnace of his power, and then hammer out upon the anvil of his skill: no, there was nothing to begin with in that day of Jehovah's work; from the womb of omnipotence all things must be born. He speaks, and the heavens leap into existence. He speaks again, and worlds are begotten with all the varied forms of life so fraught with divine wisdom and matchless skill. "Let there be light, and there was light," was not the only time when God had spoken, and when things that were not were, for aforetime had he spoken, and this rolling earth, and yon blue heavens, had blossomed out of nothingness. Through him were all things, from the high archangel who sings his praises in celestial notes, down to the cricket chirping on the hearth. The same finger paints the rainbow and the wing of the butterfly. He who dyes the garments of evening in all the colours of heaven, has covered the kingcup with gold, and lit up the glowworm's lamp. From yonder ponderous mountain, piercing the clouds, down to that minute grain of dust in the summer's threshing-floor—all things through him are. Let but God withdraw the emanations of his divine power, and everything would melt away as the foam upon the sea melts into the wave which bore it. Nothing could stand an instant if the divine foundation were removed. If he should shake the pillars of the world, the whole temple of creation falls to ruin, and its very dust is blown away. A dreary waste, a silent emptiness, a voiceless wilderness is all which remaineth if God withdraw his power; nay, even so much as this were not if his power should be withheld.

That nature is as it is, is through the energy of the present God. If the sun riseth every morning, and the moon walketh in her brightness at night, it is through him. Out upon those men who think that God has wound up the world, as though it were the clock, and has gone away, leaving it to work for itself apart from his present hand. God is present everywhere—not merely present when we tremble because his thunder shakes the solid earth, and sets the heavens in a blaze with lightnings, but just as much so in the calm summer's eve, when the air so gently fans the flowers, and gnats dance up and down in the last gleams of sunlight. Men try to forget the divine presence by calling its energy by strange names. They speak of the power of gravitation; but what is the power of gravitation? We know what it does, but what is it? Gravitation is God's own power. They tell us of mysterious laws—of electricity, and I know not what. We know the laws, and let them wear the names they have; but laws cannot operate without power. What is the force of nature? It is a constant emanation from the great Fountain of power, the constant outflowing of God himself, the perpetual going forth of beams of light from him who is "the great Father of Lights, with whom is no variableness, neither shadow." Tread softly, be reverent, for God is here, O mortal, as truly as he is in heaven. Wherever thou art, and whatever thou lookest upon, thou art in God's workshop, where every wheel is turned by his hand. Everything is not God, but God is in everything, and nothing worketh, or even existeth, except by his present power and might. " Of him, and through him, are all things."

Beloved, the great glory of all is that in the work of creation everything is *to* him. Everything will praise the Lord: he so designed it. God must have the highest motive, and there can be no higher motive conceivable than his own glory. When there was no creature but himself, and no being but himself, God could not have taken as a motive a creature which did not exist. His motive must be himself. His own glory is his highest aim. The good of his creatures he considereth carefully; but even the good of his creatures is but a means to the main end, the promotion of his glory. All things then are for his pleasure, and for his glory they daily work. Tell me that the world is marred by sin and I lament it; tell me that the slime of the serpent is upon everything beautiful here and I sorrow for it; but yet, even yet, shall everything speak of the glory of God. To him are all things, and the day shall come, when with eye spiritually illuminated, you and I shall see that even the introduction of the fall and the curse did not after all mar the splendour of the majesty of the Most High. To him shall all things be. His enemies shall bow their necks unwillingly but abjectly; whilst his people, redeemed from death and hell, shall cheerfully extol him. The new heavens and the new earth shall ring with his praise, and we who shall sit down to read the record of his creating wonders, shall say of them all, " In his temple doth everyone speak of his glory, and even until now to him have all things been." Courage, then, beloved; when you think that matters go against the cause of God throw yourselves back upon this as a soft couch. When the enemy hisseth in your ears this note—" God is overcome; his plans are spoiled; his gospel is thrust back; the honour of his Son is stained;" tell the enemy, " Nay, it is not so; *to him* are all things." God's defeats are victories. God's weakness is stronger than man, and even the foolishness of the Most High is wiser than man's wisdom, and at the last we shall see most clearly that it is so. Hallelujah!

We shall see, dear friends, one day in the clear light of heaven, that every page in human history, however stained by human sin, hath nevertheless something of God's glory in it; and that the calamities of nations, the falling of dynasties, the devastations of pestilence, plagues, famines, wars, and earthquakes, have all worked out the eternal purpose and glorified the Most High. From the first human prayer to the last mortal sigh, from the first note of finite praise onward to the everlasting hallelujah, all things have worked together for the glory of God, and have subserved his purposes. All things are of him, and through him, and to him.

This great principle is most manifest *in the grand work of divine grace.* Here everything is *of God,* and through God, and to God. The great plan of salvation was not drawn by human fingers. It is no concoction of priests, no elaboration of divines; grace first moved the heart of God and joined with divine sovereignty to ordain a plan of salvation. This plan was the offspring of a wisdom no less than divine. None but God could have imagined a way of salvation such as that which the gospel presents—a way so just to God, so safe to man. The thought of divine substitution, and the sacrifice of God on man's behalf, could never have suggested itself to the most educated of all God's creatures. God himself suggests it, and the plan is " of him." And as the great plan is of him, so the fillings up of the minutiæ are of him. God ordained the time when the first promise should be promulgated, who should receive that promise, and who should deliver it. He ordained the hour when the great promise-keeper should come, when Jesus Christ should appear, of whom he should be born, by whom he should be betrayed, what death he should die, when he should rise, and in what manner he should ascend. What if I say more? He ordained those who should accept the Mediator, to whom the gospel should be preached, and who should be the favoured individuals in whom effectual calling should make that preaching mighty for salvation. He settled in his own mind the name of every one of his chosen, and the time when each elect vessel should be put upon the wheel to be fashioned according to his will; what pangs of conviction should be felt when the time of faith should come, how much of holy light and enjoyment should be bestowed—all this was purposed from of old. He settled how long the chosen vessel should be glazing in the fire, and when it should be taken up, made perfect by heavenly workmanship, to adorn the palace of God Most High. Of the Lord's wisdom every stitch in the noble tapestry of salvation most surely comes.

Nor must we stop here; *through* him all these things come. Through his Spirit the promise came at last, for he moved the seers and holy men of old; through him the Son of God is born of the Virgin Mary by the power of the Holy Spirit; through him, sustained by that Spirit, the Son of God leads his thirty years of perfection. In the great redemption God alone is exalted. Jesus sweats in Gethsemane and bleeds on Calvary. None stood with our Saviour there. He trod that winepress alone, his own arm wrought salvation, and his own arm upheld him. Redemption-work was through God alone; not one soul was ever redeemed by human suffering, no spirit emancipated by mortal penance, but all through him. And as through him the atonement, so through him the application of the atonement. By the power of the Spirit the gospel is daily preached; upheld by the Holy Ghost, pastors, teachers, and elders, still abide with the Church; still the energy of the Spirit goeth forth with the Word to the hearts of the chosen; still is " Christ crucified;" the power of God and the wisdom of God, because God is in the Word, and through him men are called, converted, saved.

O my brethren, beyond a doubt we must confess of this great plan of salvation that it is all *to* him: we have not a note of praise to spare for another. Silenced for ever with everlasting confusion be the man who would retain a solitary word of praise for man or angel in the work of grace. Ye fools! who can be praised but God, for who but God determined to give his Son Jesus? Ye knaves! will ye rob Christ of his glory? Will ye steal the jewels out of his crown when he so dearly bought them with drops of his precious blood? O ye who love darkness rather than light, will ye glorify man's will above the energy of the Holy Spirit, and sacrifice to your own dignity and freedom?

God forgive you; but as for his saints, they will always sing, "To God, to God alone be all the glory; from the first to the last let him who is the Alpha and the Omega have all the praise; let his name be extolled, world without end." When the great plan of grace shall be all developed, and you and I shall stand upon the hill-tops of glory, what a wondrous scene will open up before us! We shall see more clearly then than now, how all things sprang from the fountain-head of God's love, how they all flowed through the channel of the Saviour's mediation, and how they all worked together to the glory of the same God from whom they came. The great plan of grace, then, bears out this principle.

The word holds good, dear friends, *in the case of every individul believer.* Let this be a matter for personal enquiry. Why am I saved? Because of any goodness in me, or any superiority in my constitution? Of whom comes my salvation? My spirit cannot hesitate a single moment. How could a new heart come out of the old one? Who can bring a clean thing out of an unclean? Not one. How can the spirit come out of the flesh. That which is born of the flesh is flesh: if it be spirit it must be born of the Spirit. My soul, thou must be quite clear about this, that if there be in thee any faith, hope, or spiritual life, it must have come of God. Can any Christian here who possesses vital godliness differ from this statement? I am persuaded he cannot; and if any man should arrogate any honour to his own natural constitution, I must, with all charity, doubt whether he knows anything at all about the matter.

But, my soul, as thy salvation must have come out of God, as he must have thought of it and planned it for thee, and then bestowed it upon thee, did it not also come to thee *through* God! It came through faith, but where did that faith take its birth? Was it not of the operation of the Holy Spirit? And what didst thou believe in? Didst thou believe in thine own strength, or in thine own good resolution? nay, but in Jesus, thy Lord. Was not the first ray of light thou ever hadst received in this way? Didst thou not look entirely away from self to the Saviour? And the light which thou now hast, does it not always come to thee in the same way, by having done once for all with the creature, with the flesh, with human merit, and resting with childlike confidence upon the finished work and righteousness of the Lord Jesus Christ? Is not, dear hearer, is not thy salvation, if thou be indeed saved, entirely "through" thy God, as well as "of" thy God? Who is it that enables thee to pray every day? Who keeps thee from temptation? By what grace art thou led onward in spiritual duty? Who upholds thee when thy foot would trip? Art thou not conscious that there is a power other than thine own? For my part, brethren, I am not taken to heaven against my will, I know, but still so desperate is my nature, and so prone to evil, that I feel myself floated onward against the current of my nature. It seems as if all we could do were to kick and rebel against sovereign grace, while sovereign grace says, "I will save thee; I will have thee, whatever thou mayst do. I will overcome thy raging corruption; I will quicken thee out of thy lethargy, and take thee to heaven in a fiery chariot of afflictions, if not by any other means. I will whip thee to paradise sooner than let thee be lost."

Is not this your experience? Have you not found that if once the strong hand of God were taken from your soul, instead of going onward to heaven you would go back again to perdition? It is *through* God you are saved. And what say you, believer, to the last point? Is it not "*to* him?" Will you take one single jewel out of his crown? Oh! there is not one of you who would wish to extol himself. There is no song we sing more sweetly in this house of prayer than the song of grace, and there is no hymn which seems more in keeping with our own experience than this—

> "Grace all the work shall crown,
> Through everlasting days ;
> It lays in heaven the topmost stone,
> And well deserves the praise."

Let who will extol the dignity of the creature; let who may boast in the power of free will, we cannot do it; we have found our nature to be a very depraved one, and our will to be under bondage. We must, if other creatures do not, extol that unchangeable omnipotent grace which has made us what we are, and will continue to keep us so till it bringeth us to the right hand of God in everlasting glory. In each individual, then, this rule holds good.

Once more, *in every work which the Christian is enabled to do*, he should bear in mind the rule of the text. Some of you are privileged to work in the Sabbath-school, and you have had many conversions in your class; others of you are distributing tracts, going from house to house, and trying to bring souls to Christ, not without success; some of us, too, have the honour of being sent to preach the gospel in every place, and we have sheaves of our harvest too many for our barns to hold. In the case of some of us, we seem to have received the promised blessing to its fullest extent; the Lord has spiritually made our children like the sand of the sea, and the spiritual offspring of our bowels like the gravel thereof. In all this it behoveth us to remember that " of him, and through him, and *to* him," are all things. " *Of* him." Who maketh thee to differ? What hast thou which thou hast not received? The burning heart, the tearful eye, the prayerful soul—all these qualifications for usefulness come of him. The fluent mouth, the pleading tongue, these must have been educated and given by him. From him all the divers gifts of the Spirit by which the Church is edified—from him, I say, they all proceed. What is Paul? Who is Apollos, or Cephas—who are all these but the messengers of God, in whom the Spirit worketh, dividing to every man according as he will? When the preacher has achieved his usefulness, he knows that all his success comes *through* God. If a man shall suppose himself capable of stirring up a revival, or encouraging even one saint, or leading one sinner to repentance, he is a fool. As well might we attempt to move the stars, or shake the world, or grasp the lightning flash in the hollow of our hand, as think to save a soul, or even to quicken saints out of their lethargy. Spiritual work must be done by the Spirit. Through God every good thing cometh to us. The preacher may be a very Samson when God is with him: he shall be like Samson when God is not with him only in Samson's degradation and shame. Beloved, there never was a man brought to God except through God, and there never will be. Our nation shall never be stirred up again into the celestial heat of piety except by the presence of the Holy Spirit anew. Would God we had more of the abiding sense of the Spirit's work among us, that we looked more to him, rested less in machinery and men, and more upon that Divine but Invisible Agent who worketh all good things in the hearts of men. Beloved, it is through God that every good thing comes; and I am sure it is *to him*. We cannot take the honour of a single convert. We do look with thankfulness upon this growing Church; but we can give the glory alone to him. Give glory to the creature, and it is all over with it; honour yourselves as a Church, and God will soon dishonour you. Let us lay every sheaf upon his altar, bring every lamb of the fold to the feet of the good Shepherd, feeling that it is his. When we go abroad to fish for souls, let us think that we only fill the net, because he taught us how to throw it on the right side of the Church, and when we take them they are his, not ours. Oh! what poor little things we are, and yet we think we do so much. The pen might say, "I wrote Milton's Paradise Lost." Ah! poor pen! thou couldst not have made a dot to an "i," or a cross to a "t," if Milton's hand had not moved thee. The preacher could do nothing if God had not helped him. The axe might cry, "I have felled forests; I have made the cedar bow its head, and laid the stalwart oak in the dust." No, thou didst not; for if it had not been for the arm which wielded thee, even a bramble would have been too much for thee to cut down. Shall the sword say, "I won the victory; I shed the blood of the mighty; I caused the shield to be cast away?" No, it was the warrior, who with his courage and might made thee of service in the battle, but apart from this thou art less than nothing. In all that God doth by us, let us continue to give him the praise, so shall he continue his presence with our efforts, otherwise he will take from us his smile, and so we shall be left as weak men.

I have, perhaps, at too great length for your patience, tried to bring out this very simple but very useful principle; and now, before I go to the second part, I wish to apply it by this very practical remark. Beloved, if this be true, that all things are through him and to him, do you not think that those doctrines are most likely to be correct and most worthy to be held, which are most in keeping with this truth? Now, there are certain doctrines commonly called Calvinistic (but which ought never to have been called by such a name, for they are simply Christian doctrines), which I think commend themselves to the minds of all thoughtful persons, for this reason mainly, that they do ascribe to God everything. Here is the doctrine of *election*, for instance, why is a man saved? Is it the result of his own will or God's will? Did he choose God, or did God choose him? The answer "Man chose God," is manifestly untrue, because it glorifies man. God's answer to it is, "Ye have not chosen me, but I have chosen you." God hath predestinated his people to salvation from before the foundation of the world. Ascribing the will, which is the hinge of the whole matter, and turns the balance—ascribing that to God, we feel we are speaking in keeping with the doctrine of our text.

Then take *effectual calling*. By what power is a man called? There are some who say that it is by the energy of his own will, or at least that while God gives him grace, it depends upon him to make use of it: some do not make use of the grace and perish, others make use of the grace and are saved; saved by their own consenting to allow grace to be effectual. We, on the other hand, say *no*, a man is not saved against his will, but he is made willing by the operation of the Holy Ghost. A mighty grace which he does not wish to resist enters into the man, disarms him, makes a new creature of him, and he is saved. We believe that the calling which saves the soul is a calling which owes nothing at all to man, but which comes from God, the creature being then passive, while God, like the potter, moulds the man like a lump of clay. Clearly the calling, we think, must be *through* God; for so it coincides with this principle " of him, and through him, and to him are all things."

Then next, the question of *particular redemption.* Some insist upon it that men are redeemed not because Christ died, but because they are willing to give efficacy to the blood of Christ. He died for everybody according to their theory. Why, then, are not all men saved? Because all men will not believe? That is to say that believing is necessary in order to make the blood of Christ efficacious for redemption. Now we hold that to be a great lie. We believe the very contrary, namely, that the blood of Christ has in itself the power to redeem, and that it does redeem, and that faith does not give efficacy to the blood, but is only the proof that the blood has redeemed that man. Hence we hold that Christ did not redeem every man, but only redeemed those men who will ultimately attain unto eternal life. We do not believe that he redeemed the damned; we do not believe that he poured out his life blood for souls already in hell. We never can imagine that Christ suffered in the room and stead of all men, and that then afterwards these same men have to suffer for themselves, that in fact Christ pays their debts, and then God makes them pay their debts over again. We think that the doctrine that men by their wills give efficacy to the blood of Christ is derogatory to the Lord Jesus, and we rather hold to this that he laid down his life for his sheep, and that his laying down his life for the sheep involved and secured the salvation of every one of them. We believe this because we hold that " of him, and through him, and to him are all things."

So, again, take the *total depravity* of the race, and its *original corruption*, a doctrine much abhorred of those who lift up poor human nature, is nevertheless true. We hold that man must be entirely lost and ruined, because if there be some good thing in him, then it cannot be said that " of God, and through God, and to God, are all things," for at least some things must be of man. If there be some relics of virtue and some remnants of power left in the race of man, then some things are of man, and to man will some things be. But if of God are all things, then in man there must be nothing—man must be set down as ruined—hopelessly ruined—

" Bruised and mangled by the fall,"

and his salvation must be described as being from the first to the last, in every jot and every tittle of that almighty grace of God, which at first chose him, at length redeemed him, ultimately called him, constantly preserved him, and perfectly shall present him before the Father's throne.

I put these doctrines before you, more especially to-day, because last Friday many believers both in Geneva and London, met together to celebrate the tri-centenary of the death of that mighty servant of God, John Calvin, whom I honour, not as teaching these doctrines himself, but as one through whom God spoke, and one who, next to the apostle Paul, propounded truth more clearly than any other man that ever breathed, knew more of Scripture, and explained it more clearly. Luther may have as much courage, but Luther knows little of theology. Luther, like a bull, when he sees one truth, shuts his eyes and dashes against the enemy, breaking down gates, bolts, and bars, to clear away for the Word; but Calvin, following in the opened pathway, with clear eye, searching Scripture, ever acknowledging that of God, and through God, and to God are all things, maps out the whole plan with a delightful clearness which could only have come of the Spirit of God. That man of God expounds the doctrines in so, excellent and admirable a manner, that we cannot too much bless the Lord who sent him, or too much pray that others like him may be honest and sincere in the work of the Lord.

Thus much then, of doctrine, but one or two minutes by way of devotion.

II.   The apostle puts his pen back into the ink bottle, falls on his knees—he cannot help it—he must have a doxology.   "To whom be glory for ever, Amen."   Beloved, let us imitate this DEVOTION.   I think that this sentence should be the prayer, the motto for every one of us— "To whom be glory for ever, Amen."

I will be but very brief, for I would not weary you.   "To whom be glory for ever."   This should be *the single* desire of the Christian.   I take it that he should not have twenty wishes, but only one.   He may desire to see his family well brought up, but only that "To God may be glory for ever."   He may wish for prosperity in his business, but only so far as it may help him to promote this—"To whom be glory for ever." He may desire to attain more gifts and more graces, but it should only be that "To him may be glory for ever."   This one thing I know, Christian, you are not acting as you ought to do when you are moved by any other motive than the one motive of your Lord's glory.   As a Christian, you are "of God, and through God," I pray you be "to God." Let nothing ever set your heart beating but love to him.   Let this ambition fire your soul; be this the foundation of every enterprise upon which you enter, and this your sustaining motive whenever your zeal would grow chill—*only, only* make God your object.   Depend upon it, where self begins sorrow begins; but if God be my supreme delight and only object,

> "To me 'tis equal whether love ordain
> My life or death—appoint me ease or pain."

To me there shall be no choice, when my eye singly looks to God's glory, whether I shall be torn in pieces by wild beasts or live in comfort— whether I shall be full of despondency or full of hope. If God be glorified in my mortal body, my soul shall rest content.

Again, let it be our *constant* desire, "To him be glory." When I wake up in the morning, O, let my soul salute her God with gratitude.

> " Wake, and lift up thyself, my heart,
> And with the angels bear thy part,
> Who all night long unwearied sing
> High praises to the eternal King."

At my work behind the counter, or in the exchange, let me be looking out to see how I may glorify him. If I be walking in the fields, let my desire be that the trees may clap their hands in his praise. May the sun in his march shine out the Master's glory, and the stars at night reflect his praise. It is yours, brethren, to put a tongue into the mouth of this dumb world, and make the silent beauties of creation praise their God. Never be silent when there are opportunities, and you shall never be silent for want of opportunities. At night fall asleep still praising your God; as you close your eyes let your last thought be, " How sweet to rest upon the Saviour's bosom!" In afflictions praise him; out of the fires let your song go up; on the sick-bed extol him; dying, let him have your sweetest notes. Let your shouts of victory in the combat with the last great enemy be all for him; and then when you have burst the bondage of mortality, and come into the freedom of immortal spirits, then, in a nobler, sweeter song, you shall sing unto his praise. Be this, then, your constant thought—" To him be glory for ever."

Let this be your earnest thought. Do not speak of God's glory with cold words, nor think of it with chilly heart, but feel, " I must praise him; if I cannot praise him where I am, I will break through these narrow bonds, and get where I can." Sometimes you will feel that you long to be disembodied that you may praise him as the immortal spirits do. I *must* praise him. Bought by his precious blood, called by his Spirit, I cannot hold my tongue. My soul, canst thou be dumb and dead? I must praise him. Stand back, O flesh; avaunt, ye fiends; away, ye troubles; I must sing, for should I refuse to sing, sure the very stones would speak.

I hope, dear friends, whilst thus earnest your praise will also be *growing*. Let there be growing desire to praise him of whom and through him are all things. You blessed him in your youth, do not be content with such praises as you gave him then. Has God prospered you in business? give him more as he has given you more. Has God given you experience? O, praise him by better faith than you exercised at first. Does your knowledge grow? Oh! then you can sing more sweetly. Do you have happier times than you once had? Have you been restored from sickness, and has your sorrow been turned into peace and joy? The give him more music; put more coals in your censer, more sweet frankincense, more of the sweet cane bought with money. Oh! to serve him every day, lifting up my heart from Sabbath to Sabbath, till I reach the ever-ending Sabbath! Reaching from sanctification to sanctification, from love to love, from strength to strength, till I appear before my God!

In closing, let me urge you to make this desire practical. If you really glorify God, take care to do it not with lip-service, which dies away in the wind, but with solid homage of daily life. Praise him by your patience in pain, by your perseverance in duty, by your generosity in his cause, by your boldness in testimony, by your consecration to his work; praise him, my dear friends, not only this morning in what you do for him in your offerings, but praise him every day by doing something for God in all sorts of ways, according to the manner in which he has been pleased to bless you. I wish I could have spoken worthily on such a topic as this, but a dull, heavy headache sits upon me, and I feel that a thick gloom overshadows my words, out of which I look with longing, but cannot rise. For this I may well grieve, but nevertheless God the Holy Ghost can work the better through our weakness, and if you will try and preach the sermon to yourselves, my brethren, you will do it vastly better than I can; if you will meditate upon this text this afternoon, " Of him, through him, and to him are all things," I am sure you will be led to fall on your knees with the apostle, and say, " To him be glory for ever;" and then you will rise up, and practically in your life, give him honour, putting the " Amen " to this doxology by your own individual service of your great and gracious Lord. May he give a blessing now, and accept your thank-offering through Christ Jesus.

4. The Saints Blessing the Lord

"Bless the Lord, O my soul: and all that is within me, bless his holy name."—
Psalm ciii. 1.

You see here a man talking to himself, a soul with all his soul talking to his soul. Every speaker should learn to soliloquise. His own soul is the first audience a good man ought to think of preaching to. Before we address ourselves to others we should lecture within the doors of our own heart. Indeed, if any man desires to excite the hearts of others in any given direction, he must first stir up himself upon the same matter. He who would make others grateful must begin by saying, "Bless the Lord, O my soul." David had never risen to the height of saying "Bless the Lord, ye his angels;" or "Bless the Lord, all his works; " if he had not first tuned his own voice to the gladsome music. No man is fit to be a conductor in the choirs of holy song until he has learned himself to sing the song of praise. "Bless the Lord, O my soul," is the preacher's preparation in the study, without which he must fail in the pulpit. Self-evident as this is, many persons need to be reminded of it ; for they are ready enough to admonish others, but forget that true gratitude to God must, like charity, begin at home. There is an old proverb which saith, " The cobbler's wife goes barefoot," and I am afraid this is too often the case in morals and religion. Preachers ought especially to be jealous of themselves in this particular, lest, whilst they are crying aloud to other men to magnify the Lord, they should be shamefully silent themselves. I would this morning glow with the sacred flame of personal thankfulness while I call upon you to bless the holy name of Jehovah, our God. But what is true of preachers is true of all other workers. The tendency among men is, when they grow a little earnest, to expend their zeal upon other people, and frequently in the way of fault-finding. It is wonderfully easy to wax indignant at the indolence, the divisions, the coldness, or the errors of the Christian church, and to fulminate our little bulls against her, declaring her to be weighed in our balances and found wanting, as if it mattered one halfpenny to the church what the verdict of our imperfect scales might be. Why, instead of a tract upon the faults of the church, at the present moment, it would be easy to write a folio volume ; and when it was written it would be wise to put it in the fire. Friend, mind those beams in your own eye, and leave the Lord Jesus to clear the motes from the eye of his church. Begin at home ; there is in-door work to be done. Instead of vainly pointing to the faults of others, pour forth thine earnestness in praising God, and say thou unto thine own heart, "Bless the Lord, O my soul : and all that is within *me*, bless his holy name."

You observe that this preacher, with an audience of one, has a very choice subject : he is exhorting himself to bless God. Now, in a certain sense it is not possible for us to bless God. He blesses us, and in the same sense we cannot bless him. He hath all things,—what can we give to him ? When we have given our best we are compelled to confess, " Of thine own have we given unto thee." But we bless him by being thankful, by extolling him for the gifts he has bestowed, by loving him in consequence of his bounty towards us, and by allowing these emotions of our mind to influence our life, so that we speak well of his name, and act so as to glorify him among our fellow men. In these ways we can bless God, and we know that he accepts such attempts, poor and feeble though they be. God is pleased with our love and thankfulness; and so, speaking after the manner of men, he is blessed by his children's desires and praises.

Note that the Psalmist stirred himself up to bless God's *name*, by which is meant his character ; though indeed we may take the word literally, for every name of God is a reason for thankfulness. We will praise Jehovah, the self-existent : we will praise El, the mighty God whose power is on our side ; we will praise him who gives himself the covenant name of Elohim, and reveals therein the Trinity of his sacred unity ; we will praise the Shaddai, the all-sufficient God, and magnify him, because out of his fulness have we all received. And whatever other name there be in Scripture, or combination of names, every one shall be exceeding delightful to our hearts, and we will bless the sacred name. We will bless the Father, from whose everlasting love we received our election unto eternal life ; the Father, who hath begotten us again unto a lively hope by the resurrection of his Son, Jesus Christ, from the dead. We bless the Father of our spirits, who hath given to us an inheritance amongst all them that are set apart. And we bless the Son of God, Jesus our Saviour, Christ,—anointed to redeem. Our heart dances for joy at every remembrance of him. There is not a name of Jesus Christ's person, or offices, or relationships, which we would forget to bless. Whether he be Immanuel, Jesus, or the Word ; whether he be Prophet, Priest or King ; whether he be brother, husband or friend ; whatever name beseems his beloved person is dear to us, and we will bless him under it. And the Holy Ghost too,—our Comforter, the Paraclete, the heavenly Dove, who dwells within our hearts in infinite condescension, whom heaven cannot contain, but yet who finds a habitation within the bodies of his servants, which are his temples—we will assuredly praise him. Each one of his influences shall evoke from us grateful praise,—if he be like the wind—we will be as Æolian harps; if he be dew—we will bloom with flowers; if he be flame—we will glow with ardour; if he be oil—our faces shall shine. In whatever way he moves upon us we will be responsive to his voice; and while he blesses us we will bless his holy name.

But if the very name of God be thus blessed to us, certainly the character which lies beneath the name shall be inexpressibly delightful. Select any attribute of God you will, and it is a reason for our loving him. Is he immutable?—blessed be his name, he loves everlastingly. Is he infinite?—then glory be to him, it is infinite affection which he has bestowed upon us. Is he omnipotent?—then will he put forth all his power for his own beloved. Is he wise?—then he will not err, nor fail to bring us safely to our promised rest. Is he gracious?—then in that grace we find our comfort and defence;—whatever there is in God, known or unknown, we will bless. My God! I cannot apprehend thee with my understanding, but I comprehend thee with my affections; and so, if I cannot know thee all in my mind, I love thee altogether in my heart; my intellect is too narrowed to contain thee, but my heart expands herself to the infinity of thy majesty, and loves thee, whatever thou mayest be. Thou art unknown in great measure, but thou art not unloved of my poor heart. Thus the Psalmist calls upon us to bless the Lord.

I would like to dwell upon that emphatic word in his exhortation—his *holy* name. Only a holy man can delight in holy things. Holiness is the terror of unholy men; they love sin and count it liberty, but holiness is to them a slavery. If we be saints we shall bless God for his holiness, and be glad that in him there is no spot nor flaw; without iniquity, just and right is he. Even to save his people he would not violate his law; even to deliver his own beloved from going down into the pit he would not turn away from the paths of equity. "Holy, holy, holy Lord God of Sabaoth," is the loftiest cry of cherubims and seraphims in their perfect bliss; it is a joyous song both to the saints on earth and those in heaven. The pure in heart gaze on the divine holiness with awe-struck joy.

Having thus expounded the words briefly, we will now come to the main point of the exhortation. The Psalmist stirs us up to bless God with our whole being, and I pray the Holy Ghost to bring us to that condition this morning. Upon that part of the exhortation we shall now dwell.

I. And our first remark shall be, that this exhortation is REMARKABLY COMPREHENSIVE. "Bless the Lord, O my soul:"—there is the unity of our nature; "and all that is within me,"—there are the diverse powers and faculties which make up the variety of our nature. The unity and the diversity are both summoned to the delightful employment of magnifying God.

First, *the unity of our nature* is here bidden, in its concentration, to yield its whole self to the praise of God. "Bless the Lord, O my soul,"—he means thereby not his lips only, not his hands upon the harp strings, not his eyes uplifted towards heaven, but his soul, his very self, his truest self. Never let me present to God the outward and superficial alone, but let me render to him the inner and the sincere; let me never bring before him merely the outward senses which my soul uses, but the soul which uses these instrumental faculties. No whitewashed sepulchres will please the Lord,—"Bless the Lord, O my soul,"—Let the true *Ego* praise him, the essential I, the vital personality, the soul of my soul, the life of my life! Let me be true to the core to my God; let that which is most truly my own vitality spend itself in blessing the Lord. The soul is our best self; we must not merely bless the Lord with our body, which will soon become worm's meat, and is but dust at its best; but with our inner, ethereal nature, which makes us akin to angels,—yea, that which causes it to be said that in the image of God we were created. My spiritual nature, my loftiest powers must magnify God,—not the voice which sings a hypocritical magnificat, but the heart which means it;—not the lips which cry Hosanna thoughtlessly,—but the mind which considers and intelligently worships. Not alone this little narrow walk of my body would I fill with song, but the infinite,—through which my spirit soars on wings of boundless thought!—I would make that shoreless region vocal with Jehovah's praise. My real self, my best self, shall bless the Lord. But the soul is also our immortal self, that which will out-last time; and, being redeemed by precious blood, shall pass through judgment and enter into the worlds unknown, for ever to dwell at the right hand of God triumphant in his eternal love. My immortal soul, what hast thou to do with spending thine energies upon mortal things? Wilt thou hunt for fleeting shadows, whilst thou art thyself most real and abiding? Wilt thou heap up bubbles, whilst thou thyself wilt endure for ever, in a life coeval with the existence of God himself, for he hath given thee eternal life in his Son Jesus? Bless the Lord then,—so noble a thing as thou art shouldst not be occupied with less worthy matters. Raise thyself on all thy wings, and like the six-winged cherubim adore thy God.

But the words suggest yet another meaning,—the soul is our active self, our vigour, our intensity. When we speak of a man's throwing his soul into a thing, we mean that he does it with all his might. We say, "There is no soul in him," by which we do not mean that the man does not live, but that he has no vigour or force of character, no love, no zeal. My intensest nature shall bless the Lord. Not with bated breath and a straitened energy will I lisp forth his praises, but I will pour them forth vehemently and ardently in volumes of impassioned song. Never serve God with a hand loath for labour, which would fain withdraw itself if it dare. If thou do thine own business in a lax fashion, yet do not God's business so. If thou go to sleep over anything let it be over thy money-making, or thy buying and selling, but evermore be awake in thy service of the Lord. "Bless the Lord, O my soul!" If ever thou art thoroughly awakened, awake now! If ever thou wast all life, all emotion, all energy, all enthusiasm, enter into the same condition again. Let every part be full of ardour, sensitive with emotion, nerved with impulse, borne upward by resolution, impelled by onward force! As Samson, when he smote the Philistines hip and thigh, used every muscle, sinew, and bone of his body in crushing his adversaries, so do thou serve God with all and every force thou hast. "Bless the

Lord, O my soul !" O God, my hand, my tongue, my mind, my heart shall all adore thee :

"Every string shall have its attribute to sing."

My united, concentrated, entire being shall bless thee, thou infinitely glorious Jehovah !

I pray you, my brethren, either do not pretend to praise God at all, or praise him with all your might. If you are Christian people, be out and out Christians or let Christianity alone. None hinder the glorious kingdom of Christ so much as these half-and-half men, who blow hot and cold with the self-same breath. My brethren, be thorough ; plunge into this stream of life as bathers do who dive to the very bottom, and swim in the broad stream with intense delight. Do this, or else make no profession.

But, then, David speaks of *the diverse faculties of our nature*, and writes, "All that is within me bless his holy name." I think the Psalm itself, if we had time to comment upon it, might suggest in succession all our mental powers and passions. For instance, when he said, "Bless the Lord, O my soul," he meant, of course, first of all let the heart bless him; for that is often synonymous with the soul. The affections are to lead the way in the concert of praise. But the psalmist intended next to bestir the memory, for he goes on to say "forget not all his benefits." May I ask you, beloved friends, now to recollect what God has done for you. Thread the jewels of his grace upon the thread of memory, and hang them about the neck of praise. Canst thou count the leaves of the forest in autumn, or number the small dust of the threshing floor ? Then, canst thou give the sum of his lovingkindnesses ? For mercies beyond count, praise him without stint. Then let your conscience praise him, for the psalm proceeds to say, "who forgiveth all thine iniquities." Conscience once weighed thy sins and condemned thee; now let it weigh the Lord's pardon and magnify his grace to thee. Count the purple drops of Calvary, and say, "Thus my sins were washed away." Let thy conscience praise the Sin-bearer, who has caused it to flow with peace like a river, and to abound in righteousness as the waves of the sea. Let thy emotions join the sacred choir, for thou hast this day, if thou art like the psalmist, many feelings of delight ; bless him "who crowneth thee with lovingkind-ness and tender mercies, and who satisfieth thy mouth with good things, so that thy youth is renewed like the eagles." Is all within you peaceful, to-day ? Sing some sweet pastoral, like the twenty-third psalm. Let the calm of your spirit sound forth the praises of the Lord upon the pleasant harp and the psaltery. Do your days flow smoothly ? Then consecrate the dulcimer to the Lord. Are you joyful, this day ? Do you feel the exhilaration of delight ? Then praise ye the Lord with the timbrel and dance. On the other hand, is there a contention within ? does conflict disturb your mind ? Then praise him with the sound of the trumpet, for he will go forth with you to the battle. When you return from the battle and divide the spoil, then "praise him upon the loud cymbals : praise him upon the high-sounding cymbals." What-ever emotional state thy soul be found in, let it lead thee to bless thy Maker's holy name.

Perhaps, however, just now your thoughts exceed your emotions, for you have been considering the providence of God as you have read the histories of nations and seen their rise and fall : you have watched the hand of God in men's lives. So also did David, and he sang, " The Lord executeth righteousness and judgment for all that are oppressed." Let thy judgment praise the Judge of all the earth ; let every day's newspaper give thee fresh matter for praise : every Christian should so read the paper, or not at all. God's praise is the true end of history ; his providence is the pith and marrow of all the stories of the empires of the past. To the man of understanding the centuries are stanzas of a divine epic, whereof the great subject is the Lord of Hosts in his excellency.

Do not forget to bring thy knowledge to thine aid in thy song. Thou hast the Scriptures, and thou hast the Spirit to teach thee their inner sense ; therefore, you can soar above David when he sang, " He made known his ways unto Moses, his acts unto the children of Israel." He hath made known his Son unto thee, and in thee, therefore glorify him. The harvests of the fields of knowledge should be stored in the garners of adoration. Even our human learning should be laid at the Lord's foot, for the vessels of the tabernacle were made of the gold which Israel brought out of the land of Egypt. We would make each rivulet of knowledge swell our gratitude. Believer, know not anything which thou canst not consecrate, or else loathe to know it. Whatever fruits, new or old, are stored in thy memory, let them be all laid up for the Beloved and none else. Knowledge should supply the spices and love the flame, and so the censer of worship should always smoke with fragrant perfume.

Be sure, too, that thy faculty of wonder be used in holy things ; let thine astonishment bless God. Thou canst not measure the distance from the east to the west, thou art lost in the immensity before thee ; but Oh, bless God with thy wonder, as thou seest thy sins thus far removed from thee. Thou canst not tell how high the heavens are above the earth, but let thine astonishment at the greatness of creation lead thee to adoration, for so great is his mercy toward them that fear him. Ah, and thy very fears, let them bow low before the Lord. Dost thou fear because thou art frail ? He remembereth that we are dust. Dost thou tremble at the thought of death ? Then praise him who spares thee, though thou art before him as a flower of the field withered by the wind when it passeth over thee. Magnify from a sense of thine insignificance the splendour of that condescending love which pities thee, even " as a father pitieth his children." As for thy hopes, sweet are their voices, let them not remain silent; as they peer into the future let them sing, for " The mercy of the Lord is from everlasting to everlasting upon them that fear him." What more could hope desire to make her rouse her choicest minstrelsy ? By-and-by we shall be where even the last verses of the Psalm will not be above our experience, for we shall see the Lord upon that throne which he has prepared in the heavens, and then we will bid angels that excel in strength, and all the heavenly ministry, to bless the Lord. Happy are we as we anticipate the day, and, filled with expectation, cry aloud, " Bless the Lord, O my soul ! "

I think you will now perceive that, if time permitted, we could bring out every single mental faculty, and show that David has given it scope, as though this psalm were the working out of a problem, and practically showed how each particular power of the soul can praise God.

Brethren, we cannot longer tarry on this point. You know, each of you, what faculty you possess in the greatest strength. I pray you use it for God. You know which phase your soul is in just now ; bless God while you are in that mood, whatever it be. "*All* that is within me," says the text,—then let it be all. Some of us have a vein of humour, and though we try to keep it under restraint it will peep out. What then ? Why let us make it bear the Lord's yoke. This faculty is not necessarily common or unclean : let it be made a hewer of wood and a drawer of water for the Lord. On the other hand, some of you have a touch of despondency in your nature : take care to subdue it to the Lord's praise. You are the men to sing those grave melodies which in some respects are the pearls of song. A little pensiveness is good flavouring. The muse is at her best when she is pleasingly melancholy. Praise God, my brethren, as you are. Larks must not refrain from singing because they are not nightingales, nor must the sparrow refuse to chirp because he cannot emulate the linnet. Let every tree of the Lord's planting praise the Lord; clap your hands, ye trees of the wood, while fruitful trees and all cedars join in his praise. Both young men and maidens, old men and children, praise the name of the Lord, each one in his peculiar note; for ye are all needful to the perfect harmony. The Lord would not have you borrow your brother's tones, but use "*all that is within you*," all that is peculiar to your own idiosyncracy, for his glory. Spend all your strength, ay, every atom of it; keep back nothing, but render *all* that is *within* you unto him. If all that is within you be the Lord's, all that is *without* you, which is yours, will also be his. All your bodily faculties will praise him, and the outer life will be all for God. Let your house praise him. Beneath its roof may there ever be an altar to the God of all the families of Israel. Let your table praise him; learn to eat and drink to his glory. Let your bed praise him;—let the bells upon the horses be holiness unto the Lord;—let the very garments that you wear, seeing they are the gifts of his charity, commend the Lord to your praise; yea, let each breath you breathe inspire a new song unto the Preserver of men. Make your life a Psalm, and be yourself an incarnate hymn—" all that is within me bless his holy name." The text is comprehensive.

II. Secondly, the suggestion of the text is MOST REASONABLE.

For, first, God has created all that is within us except the sin which mars us; every faculty, susceptibility, power or passion, is of the Lord's fashioning. It were not ours to feel, to think, to hope, to judge, to fear, to trust, to know, or to imagine, if he had not granted us the power. Who should own the house but the builder ? Who should have the harvest but the husbandman ? Who should receive the obedience of the child but the father ? To whom, then, O my soul, shouldst thou render the homage of thy nature but to him who made thee all that thou art ? Moreover, the Lord has redeemed our entire manhood. When we had gone astray, and all our faculties, like lost sheep, had taken each one its own several road of sin, Christ came into the world and redeemed our entire nature, spirit, soul and body,—not a part of the man, but our complete humanity. Jesus Christ did not die for our souls only, but for our bodies too; and though at this present "the body is dead because of sin," and therefore we suffer pain and disease, yet the spirit is already life because of righteousness, and in its life we have a sure guarantee of the quickening of our mortal bodies in the day of the adoption, to wit the redemption of our body. We shall, at the coming of the Lord, be wholly restored in body and soul by the Lord's divine power, therefore let body and soul praise him who has redeemed both by his most precious blood. My body, thou art not mine to pamper thee, thou art my Lord's to serve him, for his blood has paid thy ransom-price and secured thy resurrection. My soul, my spirit, whatever faculty thou hast, Christ's blood is on all, therefore thou art not thine own. It would be sad, indeed, even to think of having an unredeemed will or an unredeemed judgment ; but it is not so, every faculty is emancipated by a ransom. If the blood on the lintel has saved the house, then it has saved every room, and every chamber of ours should be consecrated to the Redeemer's praise.

Brethren, the Lord has given innumerable blessings to every part of our nature; we spoke of them just now, one by one, and it would be very easy to show that all our faculties are the recipients of blessing ; therefore should they all bless God in return. Every pipe of the organ should yield its quota of sound. As in an eagle every bone, muscle, and feather is made with a view to flight, so is every part of a regenerate man created for praise. As all the rivers run into the sea, so all our powers should flow towards the Lord's praise.

To prove that this is reasonable, let me ask one single question :—if we do not devote all that is within us to the glory of God, which part is it that we should leave unconsecrated ? and being less unconsecrated to God what should we do with it ? It would be impossible to give a proper answer to this question. An unconsecrated part in a believer's manhood would become a nest of hornets, or, what if I say a den of devils, out of which evils would come forth to prowl over our entire being. A faculty unsanctified would be a leprous spot, a valley of Gehennam, a Dead Sea, a lair of pestilence. To be sanctified, spirit, soul, and body, is essential to us, and we must have it, it is but our reasonable service ; all that is within us must bless God's holy name ; to withhold part of the price were robbery, to reserve part of our territory from our king, would be treason.

III. But I will not further insist that it is reasonable, for I have further to assert that it is NECESSARY. It is necessary that the whole nature bless God, for at its best, when all engaged in the service, it fails to compass the work, and falls short of Jehovah's praise. All the man, with all his might, always occupied in all ways in blessing God, would still be no more than a whisper in comparison with the thunder of praise which the Lord deserves. One of our poets used a singular expression, which the fact more than justifies. He says—

> "But ah ! eternity's too short
> To utter all thy praise."

It is so ; the whole company of God's creatures would be incapable of reflecting the whole of the divine glory; and such mercy and grace does God show to us in the gift of his dear Son, that the church militant, and the church triumphant, together are not equal to well-deserved praise. Do not, therefore, let us insult the Lord with half when the whole is not enough. Let us not bring him the tithe, when, if we had ten times as much, we could not magnify him as we should. We must, moreover, give the Lord all, because divided powers in every case lead to failure. The men who have succeeded in anything have almost always been men of one thing. He who is jack-of-all-trades is master of none; he who can do a little of this and a little of that never does much of any one thing. The fact is, there is only water enough in the brooklet of our manhood to drive one wheel, and if we divide it into many trickling runnels we shall accomplish nothing. The right thing is to dam up all our forces, and allow them to spend them-selves in one direction, and so pour them all forth upon the constantly revolving wheel of praise to God. How can we afford life to evaporate in trifles, when one aim only is worthy of our immortal being?

We who have been baptised upon profession of our faith were taught in that solemn ordinance to bless the Lord with our entire being, for we were not sprinkled here or there; but we were, in the outward sign, buried with the Lord Jesus in baptism unto death, and we were immersed into the name of the Triune God. If our baptism meant anything it declared that we were henceforth dead to the world, and owned no life but that which came to us by the way of the resurrection of Jesus. Over our heads the liquid water flowed, for we resigned the brain, with all its powers of thought, to Jesus; over the heart, the veins, the hands, the feet, the eyes, the ears, the mouth, the significant element poured itself, symbol of that universal consecration which deluges all the inward nature of every sanctified believer. My baptised brethren, I charge you belie not your profession.

Remember, beloved, this one telling argument, that Jesus Christ will have of us all or nothing; and he will have us sincere, earnest, and intense, or he will not have us at all. I see the Master at the table, and his servants place before him various meats, that he may eat and be satisfied. He tastes the cold meats, and he eats of the bread hot from the oven, but as for tepid drinks and half-baked cakes he puts them away with disgust. He will look on you who are cold, and are mourning your coldness, and he will give you heat; and he will look on you who are hot and serve him with the best you have; but of the middle-man, the lukewarm, he saith, "I will spue thee out of my mouth." Jesus cannot bear lukewarm religion; he is sick of it. The religion of this present time is much of it rather nauseating to the Saviour than acceptable to him. If Baal be God, serve him; but if God be God, serve him truly. Let there be no mockery, but be true to the core. Be thorough; throw your soul into your religion. I charge you, young man, stand back awhile and count the cost; for if you wish to give to Christ a little and to Baal a little, ye shall be cast away and utterly rejected—the Lord of heaven will have nought to do with you. Bless the Lord, then, all that is within me, for only such sincere and undivided homage can be accepted of the Lord.

IV. We must now pass on, and ask your attention yet further to the next remark : whole-hearted praise is BENEFICIAL. It is beneficial *to ourselves*. To be whole-hearted in the praise of God is to elevate our faculties. There can be no doubt whatever that many a man's powers have been debased by the object which he has pursued. Poets who might have been great poets, have missed the highest seats upon Parnassus because they have selected trivial topics or themes gross and impure, and, therefore, the best features of their poesy have never been fully developed. " Bless the Lord, O my soul," and thou wilt be a man to the fulness of thy capacity. This is the way to reach the loftiest peak of human attainment. Consecration is culture. To praise is to learn. To bless God is also of preventive usefulness to us ; we cannot bless God and at the same time idolise ourselves. Praise preserves us from being envious of others, for by blessing God for all we have, we learn to bless God for what other people have. I reckon it to be a great part of praise, to be thankful to God for making better men than myself. If we are always blessing the Lord, this will save us from murmuring ; the spirit of discontent will be ejected by the spirit of thankfulness. And this will also deliver us from indolence, for, if all our powers magnify the Most High, we shall scorn the soft couch of ease and seek the place of service, that we may bring more honour to our Master. Nothing beautifies a man like praising God. There is a bath in Germany which enamels the bathers, and, if it does not make them beautiful for ever, yet, at least, beautiful for a while ;—but to plunge our whole nature in adoration is far more beautifying. I was told by one who watched the revivals in the north of Ireland years ago, that he never saw the human face look so lovely as when it was lit up with the joy of the Holy Ghost during those times of refreshing. You know how pleasing landscapes appear when the sun shines upon them. The scenery has not half its charms till the sun " of this great world, both eye and soul," enriches the view with his wealth of colour, and makes all things glow with glory. Praise is the sunlight of life. Some of you conceal beneath a cloud of indifference all the beauty of your characters. You are like the lovely mountains of Cumberland, when they are enshrouded in mist,—little or nothing attractive is visible in you. May grace like a heavenly wind drive off the fogs of our despondency and discontent, and shed the sunlight of true praise all over our soul, and the beauty of our new-created man will be discerned. May we have many lovely praiseful Christians in this church, and may they abound in other churches also.

While whole-hearted praise is beneficial to ourselves, it is also useful to others. I am persuaded many souls are converted by the cheerful conversation of Christians; and many already converted are greatly strengthened by the holy joy of their brethren. You cannot do good more effectually than by a happy consecrated life, spent in blessing God. Imagine not that pensiveness is the fairest flower of piety. There have been, in the French church especially, eminent Christians who appear to have realised a likeness to Christ, rather in the sorrow which marred his visage, than in the joy which sustained his spirit. Jesus sorrowed that we might rejoice; we are no more to imitate him in his griefs than in his five wounds. It is truly Christian-like to rejoice in the Lord at all times. We should seek to have Christ's joy fulfilled in ourselves.

If there be anything that is cheerful, joyous, dewy, bright, full of heaven, it is the life of a man who blesses God all his days. This is the way to win souls. We shall not catch these flies with vinegar,—we must use honey. We shall not bring men into the church by putting into the window of Christ's shops, coffins, and crape, and shrouds, and standing at the door like mutes. No, we must tell the truth, and show sinners the best robe, the wedding ring, and the silver sandals of joy and gladness. We must sing—

> " The men of grace have found,
> Glory began below ;
> Celestial truths on earthly ground
> From faith and hope do grow."

I read in Thomas Cooper's " Plain Talk," a story of a class leader who was in a sad state of mind, and therefore gave out in the class the hymn—

> " Ah, whither should I go,
> Burthen'd, and sick, and faint."

No one seemed to inclined to sing, and, therefore, the leader asked a certain brother Martin to start a tune. " No, no," said Martin, " I'm neither burden'd, nor sick, nor faint, I'll start no tune, not I !" Well, then, Brother Martin," said the leader, " give out a verse yourself." Whereupon Martin, with all the power of his lungs, sang—

> " Oh for a thousand tongues to sing
> My great Redeemer's praise."

Ah, that's the hymn, my brother, keep to that. If you have not a thousand tongues, at least let the one you have continue to bless the Lord while you have any being.

V. Lastly, all this is PREPARATORY. If we can attain to constant praise now, it will prepare us for all that awaits us. We do not know what will happen to us between this and heaven, but we can easily prognosticate the aim and result of all that will occur. We are harps which will be tuned in all their strings for the concerts of the blessed. The tuner is putting us in order. He sweeps his hands along the strings; there is a jar from every note; so he begins first with one string, and then goes to another. He continues at each string till he hears the exact note. The last time you were ill, one of your strings was tuned ; the last time you had a bad debt, or trembled at declining business, another string was tuned. And so, between now and heaven, you will have every string set in order; and you will not enter heaven till all are in tune. Did you ever go to a place where they make pianos, and expect to hear sweet music ? The tuning-room is enough to drive a man mad, and in the factory you hear the screeching of saws and the noise of hammers, and you say, " I thought this was a place where they made pianos." Yes, so it is, but it is not the place where they play them. On earth is the place where God makes musical instruments, and tunes them, and between now and heaven he will put all that is within them into fit condition for blessing and praising his name eternally. In heaven, every part of the man will bless God without any difficulty. No need for a preacher there to exhort you; no need for you to talk to yourself, and say, "Bless the Lord, O my soul;" you will do it as naturally as now you breathe. You never take any consideration as to how often you shall breathe, and you have no plan laid down as to when your blood shall circulate, because these matters come naturally to you; and in heaven it will be your nature to praise God; you will breathe praise, you will live in an atmosphere of adoration, and like those angels who for many an age, day without night, have circled the throne of Jehovah rejoicing, so will you. But I will not speak much on that, or you will be wanting to be flying away to our own dear country—

> " Where we shall see his face,
> And never, never sin ;
> But from the rivers of his grace
> Drink endless pleasures in."

You must stay a little while longer in the tents of Kedar, and mingle with the men of soul-distressing Mesech; but till the day break and the shadows flee away, say unto your soul, " Bless the Lord, O my soul : and all that is within me, bless his holy name."

I wish all my hearers could do this, but some of you cannot bless God at all, and it would be idle for me to tell you to do it. You are dead in your sin. I read a story the other day of a woman convinced of her state by a singular dream. She dreamed she saw her minister standing in the midst of a number of flower pots which he was watering, and she thought that she was one of the flower-pots, but the minister passed her by, and said, " It is no use watering that plant, for it is dead." This morning I must pass by the dead plants. Oh, sinner, can you bear this ? I do not invite you to sing the believer's song of praise, can you bear to be left out ? Though I pass you by, I pray the Lord to look upon you, and say to you—Live! And ere I close, I must tell you something else, which is meant for dead sinners as well as living saints. It is this : " Believe in the Lord Jesus Christ and thou shalt be saved." God grant to you that saving faith for Christ's sake. Amen.

5. Wonders

"And praise the name of the Lord your God, that hath dealt wondrously with you."—Joel ii, 26.

In the case which is particularly mentioned in this chapter, the nation of Israel had very grievously gone astray, and therefore they were visited by a very remarkable chastisement. An unusual plague of locusts devoured all the fruit of the field, and the people were vexed with a sore famine. The day of the Lord was very terrible, and none of them could abide it. The prophet Joel was commissioned to exhort them to repentance; and if, indeed, they listened to his earnest entreaties their after history was bright with mercy. By God's good hand upon them, they were brought to repentance—they wept and cried to God; and then the same God who with his left hand had been wondrous in chastisement, was, with his right hand, equally wonderful in blessing and enriching them. He loaded their floors with wheat, and made their fats to overflow with wine and oil, and restored unto them the years which the locust had eaten, so that they ate in plenty and were satisfied and praised the name of the Lord, who had dealt wondrously with them. He dealt with them by way of wonders when he smote them, and by way of wonders when he returned to them in mercy.

It was no unusual thing for the nation of Israel to meet with wonders; they were cradled in prodigies, they grew up amid miracles, they dwelt among marvels; the history of the favoured tribes is a long list of miracles. Do you not remember how the Lord brought them out of Egypt with a high hand and with an outstretched arm, what marvellous things he did among the sons of Ham, and what wonders he wrought in the fields of Zoan? By wonders they were led out of Egypt and brought through the sea, upon whose shore they sang triumphantly, "Who is like unto thee O Lord, among the gods? Who is like thee, glorious in holiness, fearful in praises, doing wonders?" Their course in the great howling wilderness for forty years was a march of wonders. When the manna dropped from heaven and the water leaped from the rock, the Lord dealt wondrously with them. There was not a single day of the forty years which did not open and close with wonders : the day was shaded by the cloudy pillar and the night glowed with the light of the fiery cloud. Nor when the desert journey was over, did God's wonders cease. The river was divided before them. What ailed thee, O thou Jordan, that thou wast driven back? They entered into their land and began its conquest by a wonder, for the walls of Jericho fell flat to the ground : and they continued its conquest by the same marvellous power, for mighty kings fled before them, and the sun and the moon stood still while they smote the hostile armies ? When they had driven out the Canaanites, and were established in the land of promise, they sinned greatly; but what wonders of deliverance God wrought for them when they cried to him in their trouble ! You have but to remember the names of Gideon and of Barak, of Jephtha and of Samson, and you see before you wonder after wonder ! The Lord dealt wondrously with them.

In all this the Israelites were a type of true believers, for with all his chosen ones the Lord has dealt wondrously. We frequently hear the complaint that we live in an age of dulness; we have no adventures now, and events are few. Happy are we that it is so, for it has been well said : " Blessed are the times which have no history." If peace and prosperity are commonplace, long may the commonplace continue. But, indeed, no thoughtful man's life is uninteresting or barren of marvels. A life real and earnest cannot be devoid of memorable occurrences. He who thinks so must either be unspiritual, or he must be oblivious of his own inner history ; he must be like the tribes in the wilderness, of whom it is written, " They forgat the works of the Lord, and the wonders which he had showed them." Foolish people run to fiction for wonders, but gracious men can tell far greater wonders, upon which the words " NO FICTION " might be written in capital letters. The wonders which we can speak of far surpass the inventions of imagination : when we recount them we may appear unto men to dream, but in very truth no dreamer could dream after such a fashion. Speak of " Arabian Nights," English days and nights have far exceeded them in marvel. " God doeth great things past finding out, and wonders without number." I have seen a volume entitled, " The World of Wonders ; " and another named, " Ten Thousand Wonderful Things ; " the believer is within himself a world of wonders, and his life reveals ten thousand wonderful things. Mysteries, riddles, paradoxes, and miracles make up Christian experience. God hath dealt wondrously with us. Of these wonders I shall try and speak at this time, according to that precept of David—" Talk ye of all his wondrous works," and I shall dwell upon them after the following manner : first, we shall testify that *God's dealings toward us have been full of wonder, and lead us to praise him, as Jehovah our God ;* and, secondly, we shall remark that because of this, *we ought to look for wonders in the future,* and if I may speak so paradoxically it should not be wonderful to us to see wonders ; and, then,

thirdly, we shall close by observing that *in a future state, we shall yet more clearly see that Jehovah hath dealt wondrously with us.*

I. THE LORD'S DEALINGS WITH US UP TILL NOW HAVE BEEN FULL OF WONDER, AND LEAD US TO PRAISE HIM. Let us speak of what we know, and have tasted, and handled. The Lord has dealt wonderfully *toward* us. Begin at the beginning. It was no small wonder that he should love us or ever the earth was. There were many other things to exercise Jehovah's thought besides thinking upon man: "What is man, that thou art mindful of him?" And if he must needs think of man there were many kinds of thoughts that the Lord might have had towards man besides thoughts of love, yet the Lord was mindful of us and still though we be poor and needy, yet the Lord thinketh upon us. "How precious also are thy thoughts unto me, O God; how great is the sum of them!" Why were they thoughts of love? Admiring gratitude gives us the only reply. And if they must needs be thoughts of love yet it is a wonder of wonders that they should be thoughts of love to me! Each Christian will feel it to be so in his own personal case: "Why did divine love settle itself upon me?" Well might we say of our God what David said of Jonathan, "Thy love to me was wonderful." The song of the Virgin may be upon each one of our lips, "He hath put down the mighty from their seat, and hath exalted them of low degree." He hath thought of us who were inconsiderable, while the great ones of the earth have been passed by. Eternal love in its sovereignty is a marvel, and cometh from the Lord of hosts, who is wonderful in counsel and excellent in working.

That divine love should have continued faithful notwithstanding our unworthiness of it, and the provocations by which we have tried it, is another wonder. The immutability of his counsel calls for adoring wonder. Has there been a day since we have been responsible for our actions in which we have not tested the faithfulness of God by our transgressions? The children of Israel for forty years provoked God in the wilderness: were they not most sadly the prototypes of ourselves? Yet never, never has the Lord paused or changed in his love. As it is said of our blessed Redeemer, "Having loved his own who were in the world, he loved them to the end;" so is it true that "the Father himself loveth you," and rests in his love.

If the divine love be in itself a wonder, brethren, it is equally a wonder that, in consequence of this love, God should enter into covenant with us. He has promised us a thousand mercies, and he has engaged himself to the performance of those promises in a remarkable way, which increases the consolation of the promise, for he has given us his oath: "I have made a covenant with my chosen; I have sworn unto David, my servant." Now, by David is meant the Lord Jesus Christ, and God has entered into covenant with us in the person of the Son of David, a covenant ordered in all things and sure, confirmed by oath, and sealed by blood, by which he has bound himself, by his own word and oath, that in blessing, he will bless us and glorify his Son in us. Behold and wonder—the Infinite enters into covenant with the finite; the Holy engages himself to sinners. We well may sit before the Lord as David did, wrapt in astonishment, and then say from our heart of hearts, "Who am I, O Lord God, and what is my house that thou hast brought me hitherto?"

It is equally wonderful that a part of the covenant should run thus: "I will be a Father unto them, and they shall be my sons and daughters, saith the Lord God Almighty." If God wanted for sons, beside the Only-begotten, he might have chosen yon bright seraphs who outshine the sun. Why looked he here upon this ant-hill to elect a seed out of such emmets as we are? Why came he down in the person of his Son to make a match with our frail humanity? O, matchless grace, that God should adopt for his children those who were heirs of wrath even as others. Behold, of these stones, he has not only raised up children unto Abraham, but unto himself also: "Behold, what manner of love the Father hath bestowed upon us, that we should be called the sons of God."

Beloved, let us admire and wonder, that, being his sons and daughters, the Lord should stake his honour upon the bringing of us securely to heaven; for in the covenant he has pledged all his attributes for his people's security. He cannot be a glorious God, unless his people ultimately be a glorified people; he cannot be true, unless his people be kept to the end, for he has pledged his honour for their safety. Jesus has said, "I give unto my sheep eternal life, and they shall never perish, neither shall any pluck them out of my hand." Yea, the Lord himself hath declared that, "Israel shall be saved in the Lord with an everlasting salvation, they shall not be ashamed nor confounded world without end." Heaven and earth shall pass away, but God's word shall not fail; sun and moon shall cease their shining, but he will not alter the thing which hath gone forth of his lips. Hath he said, and shall he not do it? Hath he spoken, and shall he not make it good?

By shifting the kaleidoscope we shall get another view of the same matchless wonders. The Lord has acted wondrously *for* us. Having loved us and covenanted with us, he gave us his Only-begotten Son to be born in our nature, and, in that nature, to suffer even unto death! I will not attempt to show to you that this is a wonder; I believe that the angels, though they have known of the incarnation nearly these nineteen hundred years, have never ceased from astonishment for one single moment. That God, the Word, should be made flesh, and should dwell among us, and that he at last should bleed and die, excels everything that is wonderful beside. That Jesus Christ, the King of kings, should be a Servant of servants, that he who wrapt the earth in the swaddling bands of ocean and spread upon the firmament its vesture of blue, should gird himself with a towel and wash his disciples' feet, is, beyond measure, a wonder! Yet this sacred office he is virtually fulfilling every day in his perpetual intercession for his people, and in all his acts of love towards them. This is indeed dealing wondrously with us.

In the gift of the Lord Jesus we have obtained pardon, justification, sanctification. and eternal life, all of which contain a mine of wonders. Perhaps to penitent hearts the chief of all these is the forgiveness of sin, and of such sins as ours.

" Great God of wonders! all thy ways
   Are matchless, God-like, and divine ;
But the fair glories of thy grace
   More God-like and unrivall'd shine :
Who is a pardoning God like thee ?
Or who has grace so rich and free ?

In wonder lost, with trembling joy
   We take the pardon of our God ;
Pardon for crimes of deepest dye ;
   A pardon bought with Jesus' blood :
Who is a pardoning God like Thee ?
Or who has grace so rich and free ?

Having given us his Son, the Lord has also, in him, given us all things. I put these things into words and sum them up, but, indeed, there is an ocean of thought in every syllable I utter, for the Lord has given us this world and worlds to come ; he has given us earth and heaven ; he has given us time and eternity, " All are yours, and ye are Christ's, and Christ is God's." Believer, there is nothing in providence but what is yours, for, " All things work together for good to them that love God, to them that are the called according to his purpose." That which looks like evil is good to you, and the good has a goodness in it which you do not yet perceive, an inner core of excellent mercy, which will be opened up for you in due time through the abounding wisdom of God. Walk thou now abroad like Abraham of old, and lift up thine eyes to the north and to the south, and to the east and to the west, for all this hath God given thee in giving thee his Son. He hath dealt wondrously with us in this respect. He has made the angels to be our servitors, glad to wait upon us and to bear us up in their hands lest we dash our feet against a stone. Making the angels to be our servants, he has made the angels' home to be our home, only he has brightened it with special glory for us. It is not written that many mansions are prepared especially for angels, but Jesus our Lord has gone before to prepare a place for us, made ready especially for our delight. Hath he not said it—" I go to prepare a place for you ?" To crown all, he has not given us merely the angels of heaven, and heaven itself, and Jesus, to prepare a place for us, but he has given us himself to be our God, for " The Lord is my portion, saith my soul," and he hath confirmed it : " I will be their God, and they shall be my people." He hath dealt wondrously for us then.

Beloved, I shall now ask you to look at your own experience a little, you that know the Lord, when I remind you that the Lord has wrought wonders *in* us. A little while ago we were dead, he made us live ; we were loathsome lepers and he made us whole ; we were blind, he gave us sight ; we were lame, he made us leap ; we were prisoners, and he set us free ; we were condemned, and he justified us by his grace. Marvellous were the changes which he wrought in us, we marvelled while we felt them. We wondered to feel the hardness of our heart removed. Years ago, nothing could move us, neither terrors nor love could stir us ; but the Lord came and smote us as Moses smote the rock, and straightway the waters of penitence gushed out, nay, the rock itself became a standing pool. What a change the grace of God makes in the matter of repentance ; the very man who was like adamant one day, becomes like wax the other ; and he who never cared for God, nor wept for sin, loathes and abhors himself in the deepest and humblest contrition ! Then, blessed be God, another wonderful change comes over him, for the man whom you saw broken in heart for sin, unable to derive a grain of comfort from anything around him, on a sudden believes on the name of Jesus as it is brought home with power to his soul by the Holy Spirit, and straightway he wipes his eyes, and his mourning is turned to dancing. He becomes supremely happy through faith, and breaks forth with such songs as this—

> " I will praise thee every day,
> Now thine anger's turned away ;
> Comfortable thoughts arise,
> From the bleeding sacrifice."

Have not your souls at times been as hard and cold as marble, and yet on a sudden they have dissolved as ice melts in the sun ? Has not your soul been tossed up and down like the Atlantic in a rage, and yet been suddenly made smooth as a " molten looking glass " by God's wondrous hand ? Your experience within you, I am sure is a verification of the statement that Jehovah your " God hath dealt wondrously with you." What wonderful conflicts our souls have known ! What wonderful victories we have won through divine grace ! Immortal sins, as they seemed to be, have received their deadly wound : unconquerable lusts have been made to bite the dust. Our victories shall never be forgotten, but the crown of them shall be put upon the head of him who enabled us to be more than conquerors. And what wonderful revelations God has granted to us. Has he not full often poured a flood of light upon a truth we saw but dimly before, and made our spirit leap for joy ? He has opened our eyes to behold wondrous things out of his law. Why, I bear witness, that sometimes when my Lord Jesus Christ himself has been revealed in my soul, I have been unable to collect my thoughts of joy, much less to put them into language that should make them intelligible to other people ; for the glory and the beauty are transcendent, and the love and the fellowship of Christ are transporting, ecstatic, ravishing : they bear the soul away. These wonders of revelation bring with them wonders of consolation. Have we not seen Christians dying full of life ? Have we not seen them sinking in body, but soaring in soul ; sick, weak, feeble, panting for their breath, and yet full of glory, ready to burst with the new wine of the kingdom that has been poured into their frail vessels ? Have we not heard some of them sing between their groans such songs as only God's sweet love could have taught them ? The angels could sing no sweeter songs, and assuredly they know no sweeter themes ! Yes, beloved, our inner experience has been full of wonders. We have committed wonderful sins, and suffered wonderful sorrows, but we have received wonderful pardons and enjoyed wonderful raptures ; we have passed through wonderful fights, but we have gained wonderful victories : wonderful has been our darkness, but we have seen marvellous light. Coleridge has said, " that in wonder all philosophy begins, in wonder it ends, and wonder fills the interspace," truly I may say the same of all vital godliness. Another has said that, "the wise man only wonders once in his life, but that is always;" the same may be affirmed of the man made wise unto salvation. It may be true that our first wonder is born of ignorance, at any rate much of ignorance mingles with its surprise; but certainly, afterwards, our wonder becomes the parent of adoration. We wonder when we grow in grace, not because we do not know, but we wonder at what we do know of amazing love and grace. Our little children look up to the stars and think them little pinholes in the sky, and they say,

"Twinkle, twinkle, little star,
How I wonder what you are:"

but when the astronomer fits his glass to his eye, and peers upon those mighty orbs, he says with greater truth,

"How I wonder what you are!"

Man's wonder grows with his knowledge; as he wades into the river of wisdom he is less and less able to keep the foothold of calm reason, and is more and more liable to be uplifted and carried off his feet by the current. It is so with Christian experience,—the more we know of God, the more wonderful his dealings to us appear.

Now, beloved, I must ask you once again to consider that, as the Lord has dealt wondrously towards us, wondrously for us, and wondrously in us, so he has also dealt wondrously by us. What a field of battle, what a throne of victory the person of a poor child of God often becomes! Why, in this narrow plot of human clay, this little Isle of Man, this United Kingdom of soul and body, the powers of heaven and hell have mustered all their armies on many a day for conflict, and God and his grace and truth have fought with Satan in our hearts, and, blessed be God, on that battle field God has won many a victory over the allied armies of the world, the flesh, and the devil. In the plains of Mansoul, Michael and his angels have fought against the dragon and his angels, and the old dragon has been defeated and led captive. We have been garrisoned against besieging sins, delivered by force of heavenly arms from the power of our corruptions, and brought forth by sovereign grace to delight in the Lord our God. When we get to heaven we shall be "men wondered at," set for signs and wonders for ever, immortal witnesses of boundless grace. We shall publish abroad, in the celestial streets, the "deeds of infinite love," to the intent that now unto the principalities and powers in the heavenly places should be made known by the church the manifold wisdom of God, according to the eternal purpose which he purposed in Christ Jesus our Lord. Will they not— the angels—say to one another, "Here are men and women who were tempted in a thousand ways, who carried about with them bodies of sin and death, who were tried with all sorts of afflictions and passed through much tribulation—but see what they are! See how God has triumphed in them; see how he has defeated the evil one, and overcome the powers of evil; for these tempted ones have come through great tribulation, and have washed their robes and made them white in the blood of the Lamb. There is not one in whom God has been defeated;

not one in whom the eternal purpose has failed; not one in whom electing love has been baffled, not one in whom the power of Christ s blood has been ineffectual, not one unto whom the Spirit came without winning a complete victory. Let us praise our God anew and sing: 'Worthy the Lamb.'"

Our God has also wrought wondrously by some of us, fulfilling his promise, "the people that do know their God shall be strong and dc exploits." His strength has been perfect in our weakness. There be some among us whose lips have fed many, and yet they confess themselves to be emptiness itself; their word has brought life to the dead, yet in themselves they have no might; they have scattered the king's enemies, although they are by nature weak as water. God's ministers are but trumpets of rams' horns, yet when God has blown through them the blast has made the walls of Jericho to rock, and reel, and fall even to the ground: they are but lamps enclosed in earthern pitchers, and yet by them Midian has been routed. Glory be to the name of Jehovah our God for this.

Thus you see God has done wondrously by us. Praise him; praise him! Shall we pause and sing a psalm of praise now? Our time would fail for that; but O, ye people, praise him! O you that know his wonders praise him! Let the redeemed of the Lord say so, whom he hath redeemed out of the hand of the enemy; let them sacrifice the sacrifices of thanksgiving, and bless the name of the Lord: "Ye shall bless Jehovah your God, for he hath dealt wondrously with you."

> "Let the redeemed of the Lord
> The wonders of his grace record;
> How great his works! how kind his ways!
> Let every tongue pronounce his praise."

II. Our second and practical point is this: THEREFORE WE OUGHT TO EXPECT WONDERS. I shall but be able to give hints here. Do you labour this morning, any of you, under a horrible sense of your sinfulness? Do you seem to yourselves to be the blackest of all unpardoned souls, the nearest to being damned already of all living beings? Do you think that it would be the greatest wonder that was ever wrought since the world began if you were saved? Dear brother, I have a most precious thought to drop into your ear (may the Holy Ghost drop it into your heart)—"The Lord is a God of wonders: he only doeth wondrous things." He delights to find in our sin and misery, room, scope, and opportunity for wonders of grace. Cast yourself upon the mercy of our matchless God, and he will make you as much a wonder of grace as you have been a wonder of sin. Possibly some are saying "I do not feel my sin as I should; I wish I did; I feel stupid, and insensible: if I feel anything, it is only a sort of regret that I do not feel at all." My dear brother, you will be a wonder, too, if God quickens you and makes you tender of heart. In you, too, he finds scope for grace. He quickeneth the dead. He kills and makes alive, he wounds and he heals. Cry to the Lord to make you sensitive, through his wounding and killing work. If your heart is cold as ice, ask him to melt it, for it is written, " He sendeth out his word and melteth them." Is it not promised in his own covenant, " I will take away the stony heart out of your flesh, and I will give you an heart of flesh " ? The Lord of love delights to work these transformations.

Do you feel dreadfully depressed in spirit ? Have you been long so ? Are you one of those who mourn without the light of the sun ? Would it not be a great marvel if you should become one of the happiest of God's people ? It would. Therefore I believe you will be, for God delights to work wonders. Out of the innermost prison he can bring his servants. He made Paul and Silas sing in the inner dungeon, and then he brought them out. He can make you sing now and bring you out into clear full liberty, and that on a sudden and to-day : " The Lord looseth the prisoners ; the Lord openeth the eyes of the blind ; the Lord raiseth them that he bowed down." The prisoners of the Lord shall not be prisoners for ever. There is a jail delivery coming, and they shall leap for joy.

Are you lying at death's door ? Do you cry like Heman, " My soul is full of troubles : and my life draweth nigh unto the grave " ? Perhaps you are sick in body, possibly you are distracted in mind, and you are ready to die, and therefore you think that it is all over with you. What a desperate case yours seems ! It would be a wonderful thing if you should yet obtain light and comfort, would it not ? Again, let me remind you that if it would be wonderful, it is all the more probable with the Lord. He is very pitiful and full of compassion, and he delighteth in mercy. The Lord healeth the broken in heart, and bindeth up their wounds. Wonderful are his ways of consoling his mourners : great is his wisdom and prudence in devising ways to bring back his banished ones. Therefore, ascribe ye greatness unto our God, and look for much mercy. Believe in God for boundless lovingkindnesses. If I preached a little Christ for little sinners, some of you would be wise to go somewhere else ; but since I have divine warrant for preaching a great Saviour for great sinners, who is able to help us through great difficulties, and to overcome great sins ; why, he is the very Saviour for you. O, bless him, and love him, and trust him, and he will work wonders in your spirit. Possibly I speak this morning to one who has desperately backslidden. It is years ago since you knew the truth ; and you have, by your sins, fastened upon your soul fetters of iron. Well, the Lord whom you have grieved is full of compassion and can take those fetters off ; yea, he can break the gates of brass and cut in sunder the bars of iron. Wonders of deliverance can the Lord work for his imprisoned children.

"Ah," cries another, " but my case is merely a commonplace one ; there is nothing remarkable about me." My dear friend, would not it be a wonderful thing if God were to save such a commonplace and insignificant person as you are ? Well, rest in him, trust in him, and there shall be wonderful works wrought for you also ; you shall be one of the men wondered at, in whom God's grace shall be fully revealed.

Let me say in one word, if there be anything about any of you, beloved, at this time which seems to render your salvation difficult, and even impossible ; if there be anything in your case that renders it hopeless and desperate, whether it be in your temporals or your spirituals, I would recommend you to go with your case to the God of wonders, and see whether or no he does not before long make you say, " The Lord hath dealt wondrously with me." To sinners who believe in Jesus salvation is promised, and they shall have it ; and to saints who trust in the Lord deliverance is promised, and delivered they must be ; God will work ten thousand wonders, but he will never allow his promise to fall to the ground.

I would earnestly remind all God's servants that we ought to expect wonderful answers to prayer ; and we should pray as if we expected the God of wonders to hear us. We ought to expect in times of trouble to see wonderful deliverances. If we seem quite shut up, we should then be sure of escaping, for it would be a wonder if we did, and therefore God will work it. We have ground for expecting wonderful consolations if we are about to endure great troubles. We should look for wonderful joys between here and heaven : we ought to be on our watch-tower, looking for wonderful discoveries of Christ's beauties and God's love ; in fact we should be always looking for wonders, and should wonder if wonders do not happen.

In the church we are permitted to expect wonders. We are too much in the habit of going to the assembly for worship, and sitting down and hearing sermons, and if half-a-dozen are converted we are astonished ; but we ought to expect thousands to be converted ! If the church ever has faith enough to expect great things, she will see great things. When the church falls upon dark times, and error mars her beauty, we may expect God to work wonders to purify and exalt her. In the darkest mediæval times God found his witnesses, and when the light threatened to die out, then Luther came, a man raised up of God, and a train of glorious men followed behind him. Never tremble, never despair, never be afraid. " The God of hosts is with us, the God of Jacob is our refuge." Why, brethren, we worship the God of wonders, " Who only doeth wondrous things." We have a Saviour of wonders. Is not his name called The Wonderful ? and did not Stephen say of him, " Jesus of Nazareth, a man approved of God among you by signs and wonders " ? Then the Holy Spirit also works wonders. He came at first with rushing wind, and cloven tongues and gifts miraculous, and even now his wonders have not ceased : they have only become spiritual, instead of physical, but the Spirit of God is working mightily now. I bear my own personal witness that God has worked wonders for us, far beyond all human ability, wonders which we could not perform ; nay, wonders that we did not deserve : what is more, wonders that we could not have expected ; what is more, wonders that we could not have imagined ; what is more, wonders which even now that they have happened we cannot comprehend ; and I may add, wonders which throughout eternity we shall never be able to praise God sufficiently for, though we spend our whole existence in wondering and adoring the wonder-working God ! " How great are his signs ! How mighty are his wonders ! His kingdom is an everlasting kingdom, and his dominion from generation to generation."

III. Our last remark is this, that IN THE FUTURE STATE THESE WONDERS WILL BE MORE MANIFEST TO US. If we were to read our Bibles attentively, we should be astonished to find how much there is about heaven in them, and how after all it is not true that we have mere gleams and glimpses, for if studiously investigated the word of God tells us wondrous things concerning the world to come. Beloved, we shall, in the better land, wonder more than we do here, for we shall there understand far more than we do now, and shall have clearer views and wider prospects. Our present capacities are narrow, there is scant room within our mind for great things; but in yon bright world the veil shall be taken off, and we shall know even as we are known, seeing no more in part and through a glass darkly: in the heavenly mansions our growing knowledge will excite in us increasing wonder, and we shall sing there the praise of him who hath dealt wondrously with us. I believe the poet was right when he said :—

> " And sing with wonder and surprise
> Thy lovingkindness in the skies."

In the abodes of endless bliss we shall see what we escaped; we shall look down from Abraham's bosom and see the sinner afar off in torment! It will be a dreadful sight, but O, with what hearts of gratitude shall we bless redeeming love, knowing each one of us that were it not for grace divine that fate so desperate had been ours. In the heaven of perfect holiness we shall know the true character of sin. When we shall see the brightness of God's glory, and the splendour of his holiness, sin will appear in all its hideousness, and we shall adore that matchless mercy which pardoned us, and bless the precious blood which cleansed us though we had been defiled with such pollution. We think we praise God for forgiving our iniquities, and no doubt we do in some measure, but, compared with the blessing that saints in heaven render to God for deliverance from sin, our praise is as nothing. We do not know sin as they know it: we do not understand its blackness as they perceive it.

Up in heaven, too, we shall see our life as a whole, and we shall see God's dealings with us on earth as a whole. A great many matters which now appear mysterious and complex, concerning which we can only walk by faith, for our reason is baffled, will be so clear to us as to excite our joyous songs in heaven. "Now I see why I was laid aside when I wanted to be busy in God's work : now I see why that dear child, whom I hoped to have had spared to me as a stay for my old age, was taken away; now I understand why my business was suffered to fail; now I comprehend why that foul mouth was allowed to be opened against me; now I comprehend why I was assailed with inward fears, and was suffered to go tremblingly all my days." Such will be our confessions when the day dawns and the shadows flee away. Then we shall say and sing : " He hath dealt wondrously with us." We shall feel that the best was done for us that even Eternal Wisdom could devise, and we shall bless the name of the Lord.

Reflect a moment, dear friends and see further reasons for everlasting wondering. In heaven we shall see what God has lifted us up to be. We talk of being sons of God. Did we ever realise that? We speak of heaven being ours : but do we know what we mean by that language? Truly " it doth not yet appear what we shall be," neither hath eye seen or ear heard the things which God hath prepared for

them that love him. When we shall stand on the sea of glass and
hear the harpers, and join their endless music ; when we shall see him
who laid down his life for us—yea, see him as he is ; when we shall
behold the Lamb of God, who by his bowing to death, lifted us up
from our deadly fall—who by stripping himself of his royalties robed us
with splendours—we shall be amazed, astounded, overwhelmed with
wonder !

Above all, when we shall see God himself, what will be our
wonder !   When our minds shall be able to behold the Infinite
Jehovah, and hear his voice, when we shall be brought to speak
with God familiarly, and bow before that throne whose brightness to-
day would blind us, if we could gaze upon it ; when we shall know him
who filleth all in all ; I will not say we shall be amazed to think he
loved us, there is no need to say that :   I will not say we shall be filled
with astonishment to think he ever saved us, I need not say that ;
but that he should permit us to be his sons and daughters, and should,
at such an expense, bring us to dwell with himself for ever, and make
us partakers of his own nature, one with his own Son—this will plunge
us in adoring wonder for ever, and we shall "praise the name of
Jehovah our God, who hath dealt wondrously with us."   I beg you to
begin the music here.   I long myself to spend my time perpetually
in adoring the God of wonders.   I want, brethren, that we should rise
above the spirit of discontent, the spirit that finds fault, and mourns,
and moans, and laments, and makes Massahs and Meribahs by which
to provoke the Lord our God.   Let it not be said of us, "They soon
forget his wonders ;" but let us go on singing unto him, "who only
doeth wondrous things," speaking to one another of all his wondrous
works, and in our souls day by day and hour by hour admiring our God,
world without end.   Amen.

6. Our Lord Before Herod

"And when Herod saw Jesus, he was exceeding glad: for he was desirous to see him of a long season, because he had heard many things of him; and he hoped to have seen some miracle done by him. Then he questioned with him in many words; but he answered him nothing."—Luke xxiii. 8, 9.

AFTER Pilate had declared to the chief priests and scribes that he found no fault at all in Jesus, they were afraid that their victim would escape, and therefore their fury was raised to the highest pitch, and they cried out the more vehemently against him. In the course of their outcries they made use of the word "Galilee;" going, as it seems to me, a little out of their way in order to drag in the name: "He stirreth up the people, teaching throughout all Jewry, beginning from Galilee to this place." Galilee was a region held in very great contempt, and they mentioned it to cast a slur upon our Lord, as if he were a mere boor from among the clowns of Galilee. To Pilate they thought that the mention of the name would, perhaps, act like the proverbial red rag held before an infuriated bull; for he appears to have been troubled by seditious persons from that province. We all remember that they were Galileans whose blood Pilate had mingled with their sacrifices. The Galileans were reputed to be an ignorant people, apt to be led astray by impostors, and so enthusiastic that they ventured their lives against the Romans. The priests would not only cast contempt upon Jesus, whom they were wont to call the Galilean, but also excite the prejudices of Pilate, so that he might condemn him to die as one of a nest of rebels.

They were mistaken, however, in the consequences of their device, for Pilate caught at the word "Galilee" directly. That province was not immediately under his rule; it was under the sway of the tetrarch Herod Antipas, and therefore he thought within himself, "I can kill two birds with one stone: I can get rid of this troublesome business by sending this prisoner to Herod, and I can also greatly gratify the king by showing him this attention." Pilate had quarrelled with Herod, and now for some purpose of his own he resolved to patch up a friendship by pretending great deference to his sovereign powers by sending one of his subjects to be tried by him. Pilate, therefore, asked, "Is this man a Galilean?" and when they told him that he was so,—for he was so, by repute, his birth at Bethlehem having been wilfully ignored,—then Pilate at once commanded that he be led to Herod, for Herod was in his palace at Jerusalem attending the Passover festival.

See, then, my brethren, our divine Master conducted in his third march of sorrow through Jerusalem. First, he was led from the garden to the house of Annas, then he was conducted through the streets from the hall of Caiaphas to the judgment hall of Pilate, and now by Pilate's orders he is led a third time by the angry crowd of priests through the streets to the palace of Herod, there to await his fourth examination. Certain of the old writers delight to remark that as there were four evangelists to do honour to our Lord, so were there four judges to do him shame. Annas and Caiaphas, Pilate and Herod. We are on safer ground when we observe with the early church the coalition of the heathen and the Jews: "For of a truth against thy holy child Jesus, whom thou hast anointed, both Herod, and Pontius Pilate, with the Gentiles, and the people of Israel, were gathered together, for to do whatsoever thy hand and thy counsel determined before to be done."

This morning I shall endeavour to set forth this portion of the sad narrative under two heads, which will be these: *Herod before Jesus,* and *Jesus before Herod.*

I.   I call your attention first to HEROD BEFORE JESUS, because you must know something of his character, something of the meaning of his questions, before you can rightly understand the sorrow which they caused to Jesus our Lord and Master.

This Herod Antipas was the son of the old Herod the Great, who had put to death the babes at Bethlehem in the hope of destroying the King of the Jews. He was a chip of the old block, but still he was several degrees baser than his sire. There was nothing of the grandeur of his father about him: there was the same evil disposition without the courage and the decision. He did not in some things out-Herod Herod, for in certain points he was a more despicable person. Herod the Great may be called a lion, but our Lord very descriptively called this lesser Herod a fox, saying, "Go and tell this fox." He was a man of dissolute habits and frivolous mind ; he was very much under the sway of a wicked woman, who destroyed any little good there might have been in him: he was a lover of pleasure, a lover of himself, depraved, weak, and trifling to the last degree. I almost grudge to call him a man, therefore let him only be called a tetrarch.

This petty tetrarch had once been the subject of religious impressions. These Herods all more or less felt the influence of religion at times, though they were by no means benefited thereby. The impressions made upon his conscience by John did not last with Herod. They were at first powerful and practical, for we are informed that " Herod feared John, knowing that he was a just man and an holy, and observed him ; and when he heard him, he did many things, and heard him gladly." I suppose he reformed many matters in his kingdom, and cast off perhaps some of his grosser vices ; but when at last John began to denounce him for having taken his brother's wife to be his paramour, while yet the brother lived, he cast his reprover into prison, and then you remember how, with reluctance, Herod, to please his mistress, beheaded John in prison.   Mark this: probably there is no more dangerous character living than a man who has once come under religious influences so as to be materially affected by them, and yet has broken loose and cast off all fear of God. He has done despite to his conscience so violently that henceforth he will know few qualms. In such a man is fulfilled the saying of our Lord " When the unclean spirit is gone out of a man, he walketh through dry places, seeking rest, and findeth none. Then he saith, I will return into my house from whence I came out ; and when he is come, he findeth it empty, swept, and garnished. Then goeth he, and taketh with himself seven other spirits more wicked than himself, and they enter in and dwell there : and the last state of that man is worse than the first." The mind of Herod Antipas was in the condition of the chamber which has been swept and garnished, for his life had been somewhat reformed, but the unclean spirit with the terrible seven had come back to his old den, and now he was a worse man by a great deal than he had ever been before. The dog returned to his vomit, and the sow that was washed to her wallowing in the mire. This Herod was an Idumæan, that is to say, one of the descendants of Esau, an Edomite, and though he had professedly become a Jew, yet the old blood was in him, as it is written concerning Edom, " He did pursue his brother with the sword, and cast off all pity." The true Jacob stood before one of the seed of Esau, a tetrarch, profane and worldly like his ancestor, and scant was the pity which he received. Esau was descended from Abraham according to the flesh, but with Jacob was the covenant according to the spirit : it bodes no good to the spiritual seed when it comes even for a moment under the power of the carnal seed. We see how the child of the flesh takes to mocking, while the child according to promise is called to patience.

Herod was in such a state of mind that he furnishes me with a typical character which I would use for the instruction and admonition of you all. He is a type of some who frequently come to this Tabernacle, and go to other places of worship occasionally,—people who were once under religious impressions, and cannot forget that they were so, but who will never be under any religious impressions again. They are now hardened into vain curiosity : they wish to know about everything that is going on in the church and kingdom of Christ, but they are far enough from caring to become part and parcel of it themselves. They are possessed with an idle curiosity which would lift the golden lid of the ark, and intrude behind the veil. They like to gather together all the absurd stories which are told about ministers and to retail all the odd remarks that were ever made by preachers for centuries. All the gossip of the churches is sure to be known to them, for they eat up the sins of God's people as they eat bread. It is not likely that their knowledge of religious things will be of any use to them, but they are ever eager after it ; the church of God is their lounge, divine service is their theatre, ministers are to them as actors, and the gospel itself so much play-house property. They are a sort of religious Athenians, spending their time in nothing else than in hearing some new thing : hoping that perhaps some singular and unexpected discourse may be delivered in their hearing which they can retail in the next company where they would raise a laugh. To them preaching is all a farce, and, worked up with a few falsehoods of their own, it makes excellent fun for them, and causes them to be regarded as amusing fellows. Let them look at Herod, and see in him their leader, the type of what they really are or may soon become.

First, let us see *idle curiosity at its best*. Look here, sirs, and then look in a glass and trace the likeness.

To begin with, we find that Herod's curiosity had been created in him by his having heard many things concerning Jesus. How did he come to hear of him? His great deeds were common talk: all Jerusalem rang with the news of his miracles and wondrous words. Herod, a convert to the Jewish faith, such as he was, took interest in anything that was going on among the Jews, and all the more so if it touched upon the kingdom, for the jealousy which set his father in a rage was not altogether absent in his son. No doubt also he had heard of Christ from John. John would not long have preached to Herod without using his own grand text, "Behold the Lamb of God, which taketh away the sin of the world." I am sure that, though he was a preacher of righteousness, he had not left off being the herald of the coming Saviour, and so from the stern lips of the great Baptist Herod had heard concerning the King of the Jews, and something concerning his kingdom. When John was dead Herod heard still more of Christ, so that, astonished with what was being done, he said, "This is John the Baptist whom I have beheaded: he is risen from the dead." Jesus became a kind of nightmare to his conscience: he was disturbed and alarmed by what he heard that the prophet of Nazareth was doing. Besides that, there was one in his household who doubtless knew a great deal about the Saviour; for in Herod's court was the husband of a woman who ministered unto the Lord of her substance. The lady's name was Joanna, and her husband was Chuza, Herod's steward —I suppose Herod's butler and manager of his household. From Chuza he could readily have learned concerning Jesus, and we may be sure that he would enquire, for the fear of the great prophet was upon him. Thus Herod's curiosity had been excited about our Lord Jesus Christ for a considerable time, and he longed to see him. I am not sorry when this happens to any of my hearers : I am right glad that they should hear something about the Lord from his friends, something about him from his ministers, and from those of us whose highest glory it is that, though we are not worthy to unloose the latchets of his shoes, yet it is all our business here below to cry, "Behold the Lamb!" So these rumours, this talk, these admonitions, had begotten in Herod's mind the desire that his eyes should light on Jesus ; so far, so good. Often men at this day come up to the house of prayer that they may hear the preacher ; not because they want to be converted, not because they have any idea of ever becoming followers of Jesus, but because they have heard something about true religion which excites their curiosity, and they would know what it is all about ; they are fond of curiosities of literature, and so they would study curiosities of religion, oddities of oratory, and things remarkable of a theological kind.

It is said of Herod, in consequence of this curiosity, that he rejoiced to see Jesus. It is said that he was " exceeding glad." What a hopeful state to be in ! May we not expect great things when a man sees Jesus

and is exceeding glad ? As I read this passage to myself, I thought,
Why, the language might well describe a child of God ; our text
might fitly be spoken concerning ourselves ; let me read it line by line,
and remark upon it. "When Herod saw Jesus, he was exceeding glad ;"
so were the apostles when Jesus manifested himself to them ; for it is
written, "Then were the disciples glad when they saw the Lord."
What other sight could bring to a true believer such joy ? "For he
was desirous to see him." Are we not ? Are not all his people longing
for that blessed vision which will make their heaven throughout
eternity ? "For he was desirous to see him of a long season." This is
also true of us : our hearts are weary with watching, and our eyes fail for
the sight of his face. "Why tarries he ?" we cry. "Make haste, my
beloved, and be thou like to a roe or to a young hart upon the mountains
of spices." "Because he had heard many things of him ; and he hoped
to have seen some miracle done by him." This, also, is our hope : we
would both see and feel some gracious miracle,—upon our eyes, that
they may be opened ; or upon our hands, that we may have greater
power in the Master's work ; or upon our feet, that we may run in the
ways of obedience ; and especially upon our hearts, that we may be ever
soft and tender, pure and gracious, to feel the mind of God. Yes, these
words read very prettily indeed ; but yet, you see, the meaning was
not the high and spiritual one which we could put into them, but the
low and grovelling one, which was all that Herod could reach.
He was "exceeding glad ;" but it was a frivolous gladness, because
he hoped that now his curiosity would be satisfied. He had Jesus in
his power, and he hoped now to hear some of the oratory of the prophet
of whom men said, "Never man spake like this man." He hoped to
see him work a miracle, even he, of whom the record was, "He hath
done all things well." Could not the great prophet be induced to mul-
tiply loaves and fishes? Might he not persuade him to heal a blind
beggar, or make a lame man leap as a hart? Would not a miracle
make rare mirth in Herod's palace, and cause a new sensation in the
mind of the worn-out debauchee? If, for instance, a corpse were dug
up, and Jesus would restore it to life, it would be something to tell of
when next the king sat down to a drinking bout with Herodias and
her like. When each was trying to exceed the other in telling strange
tales Herod would match them all! In this style many people come to
hear the gospel. They want to have an anecdote of their own about a
notorious preacher, and if they do not see something ludicrous, or hear
something striking, they will invent a tale, and swear that they
heard it and saw it, though the lie might well choke them. They act
thus because they come to hear for nothing but to feed their hungry
curiosity. None carry this to such an extreme as those who did at one
time feel a measure of the power of the word of God, but have shaken
it off. These are the mockers whose bands are made strong ; these are
the idlers who turn even the testimony of the Lord into food for mirth.
Still, at the first blush, there is something that looks very hopeful
about them, and we are pleased that they exhibit such gladness when
Christ is set forth before them.

One ill sign about Herod was the fact that his conscience had gone to
sleep after having for awhile troubled him. For a little he had been

afraid of Jesus, and trembled lest John had risen from the dead ; but that fear had subsided, and superstition had given way before his Sadducean scepticism. He hoped that Jesus would perform some wonderful thing in his presence ; but he had lost all dread of the Just and Holy One. He was a man of vain mind: the man whom he feared one day he murdered the next, and he whom he welcomed with gladness, he hurried off with derision. There was left to Herod no feeling towards Jesus but the craving after something new, the desire to be astonished, the wish to be amused. I think I see him now, sitting on his throne, expectant of wonders, like the trifler that he was. "Now we shall see," saith he, "now we shall see what we shall see ! Perhaps he will deliver himself by sheer force ; if he walked the sea, he will probably fly away in the air. Perhaps he will render himself invisible, and so pass away through the midst of the chief priests. I have heard that many a time when they would have stoned him or cast him down from the brow of a hill, he departed, gliding through their midst : perhaps he will do the same this morning." There sits the cunning prince, divining what the wonder will be ; regarding even displays of divine power as mere showman's tricks, or magician's illusions.

When Jesus was set before him he began to ask him questions : "Then he questioned with him in many words." I am glad the questions are not recorded: they could have done us no good; and, besides, our modern Herods nowadays are great masters of the art, an I need not that any man teach them. We need not to be furnished with the old-fashioned quibbles and questions ; for the supply is quite equal to our requirements. Fools can ask more questions in ten minutes than wise men are able to answer in fifty years. I say we do not want the old questions, but I daresay they would run somewhat in this line, "Are you that King of the Jews whom my father strove to slay ? How came you to be a Nazarene ? Have you been a miracleworker, or is it all legerdemain or necromancy ? John told me something about you ; did you deceive him, or is it true ? Have you raised the dead ? Can you heal the sick ?" Trying all the while to excite him to work a miracle, he raised doubts and chopped log c volubly, for the text suggestively mentions his "many words." The curious in religion are generally very apt at question-asking ; not that they want Christ, not that they want heaven, not that they want pardon of sin, not that they want any good thing ; but still they would like to know everything that is dark and mysterious in theology ; they would like to have a list of the difficulties of belief, a catalogue of the curiosities of spiritual experience. Some men collect ferns, others are learned upon beetles, and these persons pry into church life, its doctrines, pursuits, aims, and infirmities,—especially the latter. They could write a book upon orthodox England and unorthodox England, and dwell with unction upon mental vagaries. It furnishes them with something new, and adds to their store of information, and so they spare no prying questions; for they would analyze manna from heaven, and distil the tears of Christ: nothing is sacred to them ; they put Scripture on the rack, and cavil at the words of the Holy Ghost.

Thus have I set forth idle curiosity in its better stage. Now let us pass on and see how Jesus treated this curiosity, considering it under the head of IDLE CURIOSITY DISAPPOINTED. "He questioned with him in many words, but he answered him nothing !" If Herod had wanted to believe, Jesus would have been ready enough to instruct; if Herod had possessed a broken heart, Jesus would have hastened with tender words to bind it up ; if Herod had been a candid enquirer, if his doubts had been sincere and true, the faithful and true Witness, the Prince of the kings of the earth, would have been delighted to speak with him. But Jesus knew that Herod would not believe in him and would not take up his cross and follow him ; and therefore he would not waste words on a heartless, soulless profligate. Had he not said to his own disciples, "Give not that which is holy unto the dogs, neither cast ye your pearls before swine"? He saw in this man one so mean, cunning, cowardly, and heartless, that he viewed him as a fox to be let alone rather than a lost sheep to be sought after. He was a tree twice dead, and plucked up by the roots. All the Master did was to maintain an absolute silence in his presence ; and, let him question as he might, "he answered him nothing."

Observe, my brethren, that our Lord Jesus Christ came not into this world to be a performer : he did not leave his glory to earn the wondering approbation of men ; and as Herod regarded him as a mere wonderworker, and would have turned his court into a theatre wherein Jesus should be the chief actor, our Lord very wisely held his peace and did nothing at all. And sometimes his ministers might be wise if they were silent too. If they know that men have no desire to learn, no spiritual wish or aspiration, I say they might be wise if they held their tongue altogether. I have sometimes admired George Fox, who, on one occasion, when the crowd had gathered round him, expecting him to deliver some fiery address, stood still by the space of two hours while they clamoured that he would speak. Never a word did they get from him. He said he would famish them of words ; for words were all they wanted, and not the power of the Spirit. Probably they recollected his silence better than they would have remembered his most vehement discoursing. Sometimes silence is all that men deserve, and the only thing which in any probability will impress them. As the Lord Jesus was no performer, he did not gratify Herod, but answered him not a word.

Moreover, be it recollected that Herod had already silenced the Voice, and no marvel that he could not hear the Word. For what was John ? He said, "I am the voice of one crying in the wilderness." What was Jesus but the Word ? He that silences the Voice may well be denied the Word. Had not his shallow soul been moved,—I was about to say, to its depths, such depths as they were ? Had he not been admonished by one of the greatest of the children of men ? For among them that were born of women there had not then been a greater than John the Baptist. Had not a burning and shining light shone right into his very eyes ? And if he refused to hear the greatest of the sons of men, and to see the brightest light that God had then kindled, it was but right that the Saviour should refuse him even a ray of light, and let him perish in the darkness which he had himself created. Ah, sirs, you cannot trifle with religious impressions with impunity. God thinks it no trifle. He who has once been moved in his soul and has put away the heavenly word from him, may fear that it will be said of him, "My Spirit shall not always strive with man. Ephraim is joined to idols : let him alone." May not some conscience here, if it has but a little life in it, be alarmed at the memory of former rejections of the gospel, frequent quenchings of the Spirit, repeated tramplings upon the blood of Jesus ? If God never speaks to you again in the way of mercy, you have no right to expect that he should do so ; and if from this day to the day of judgment the Lord should never give you another word of mercy, who shall say that you have been treated harshly ? Have you not deserved it at his hands as Herod had done ?

Furthermore, recollect that Herod might have heard Christ hundreds of times before if he had chosen to do so. Jesus was always to be found by those who desired to listen to him. He did not go sneaking about Galilee, or holding secret conventicles in holes and corners. He ever spake in the synagogue, and Herod might have gone there ; he spake in the street or by the seashore, or on the mountain side, and Herod might have gone there. Jesus stood out boldly before the people, and his teaching was public and free ; if Herod had wished to hear him, he might have done so times beyond number : therefore now, having despised all these opportunities, the Saviour will not furnish him with another, which he would have treated in the same manner. He answers him nothing, and by so doing answered him terribly. Beware how you waste opportunities. Dear hearers, beware how you waste your Sabbaths. There may come a day when you would give a thousand worlds for another Sabbath, but it shall be denied you. There may come a day when you would count out all your wealth to have another invitation to Christ, but it will be denied you ; for you must die, and the voice of mercy will never ring in your ears again. They that will not when they may, shall not when they would. Many will knock after the Master of the house has risen up and shut to the door; but when he shutteth, no man openeth. The door was shut on Herod.

Observe, that our Master had good reason for refusing to speak to Herod this time, over and above what I have mentioned ; because he would not have it supposed that he yielded to the pomp and dignity of men. Jesus never refused an answer to the question of a beggar ; but he would not gratify the curiosity of a king. Herod dreams that he has a right to ask whatever impertinent questions he may choose to invent ; but Jesus knows nothing of men's rights in such a matter : it is all grace with him, and to him the prince upon the throne is not an atom better than the peasant in the cottage, and so when Herod in all his pride and glory thinks full sure that Christ will pay deference to him and, perhaps, will pay him court to win his favour, Jesus disregards him. He wants nothing of the murderer of John the Baptist. Had Herod been the poorest and most loathsome leper throughout all Judea, had he been the meanest mendicant in the street, who was lame or blind, his voice would at once have been heard by the Lord of mercy ; but he will not answer the prince who hopes for homage at his hands. nor feed the idle wishes of a crafty reprobate. What favour did he want at Herod's hand ? He had not come to be set free ; he had come to die, and therefore his face is set like a flint, and, with heroic courage, he answers him not a word.

Now, then, you have seen frivolous curiosity at its best, and you have seen it disappointed, as it generally is to this day. If people come to hear the gospel out of this frivolous curiosity, they usually retire saying, "Really, I do not see anything in it. We have heard nothing eloquent, nothing profound, nothing outrageous." Just so; there is nothing in the gospel to please the luxurious, though everything to bless the poor. Jesus answered Herod nothing, and he will answer you nothing if you are of Herod's order. It is the doom of triflers that they should get no answer from the gospel: neither the Scriptures, nor the ministry, nor the Spirit of God, nor the Lord Jesus will speak with them.

What was the result of this disappointment upon Herod? *Idle curiosity curdles into derision.* He thinks the man is a fool, if not an idiot, and he says so, and begins to deride him. With his men of war he mocks him, and "set him at nought," which signifies to make nothing of him. He calls his soldiers and says, "Look at this creature: he will not answer a word to what I have to say: is he bereft of his senses? Rouse him up, and see." Then they mock and laugh and jest and jeer. "Here," says Herod, "he calls himself a king! Bring out one of my shining white robes, and put it on him: we will make a king of him." So they put it about his blessed person, and again heap contumely upon him. Was it not strange—this decking him in a gorgeous robe of dazzling white? The mediæval writers delight to dwell on the fact that Herod arrayed our Lord in white and afterwards Pilate clothed him in red. Is he not the Lily of the valley and the Rose of Sharon? Is he not matchlessly white for innocence, and then gloriously red in his atoning blood? Thus, in their very mockery, they are unconsciously setting forth to us both his spotless holiness and his majestic royalty. When they had insulted to their full, they sent him back to Pilate, kicking him from foot to foot at their pleasure, as if he were a football for their sport. Then our Lord made his fourth sorrowful march through the streets of the city over which he had wept.

That is what idlers in the long run do with Christ; in their disappointment they grow weary of him and his gospel, and they cry, "Put him away; there is nothing in him, nothing of what we looked for, nothing to satisfy curiosity, nothing sensational; take him away." Away goes Jesus, never to return; and that is the end of Herod, and the end of a great many more.

II. My time is nearly gone; but bear with me while for a few minutes I try to set forth JESUS IN THE PRESENCE OF HEROD. Although no blows are recorded, I greatly question whether our Divine Master suffered anywhere more than he did in the palace of Herod. You and I, perhaps, apprehend most easily the woe of the coarser sufferings when they scourged him and when they plaited the crown of thorns and put it upon his head, but the delicate and sensitive mind of our Master was, perhaps, more touched by what he suffered in the palace of Herod than by the rougher torture. For, first, here is a man fully in earnest for the salvation of our souls, and in the midst of his grievous passion he is looked upon as a mountebank and a mere performer, who is expected to work a miracle for the amusement of an impious court. How it cuts an earnest man to the quick when he finds that, let him do what he may, people do not sympathise with him in earnestness, but are coolly criticizing his style, or imitating his mannerisms, or admiring his expressions as matters of literary taste. It is heart-breaking when your ardour makes you self-forgetful to find others pecking at trifles, or making your efforts into a kind of show. The Christ must have been wounded in his very soul when he was treated as a mere performer, as if he had left the Father's bosom and was about to give himself to death, and yet was aiming to amuse or to astonish. I know how it saddens my Lord's servants when they preach their very hearts out to bring men to repentance, and the only result is to elicit the remark that " his arguments were very telling, and that pathetic passage was very fine." There is a thorn in such chill words to pierce deeper than the crown of thorns : horrible indifference smites like the Roman scourge.

Then to think of our Lord's being questioned by such a fop as Herod ! A man of earnest and intense soul, living for one thing only, and that the redemption of mankind, is here worried by the foolish questions of a man of the world. Were you ever in an agony of bodily pain yourself, and did some frivolous person call upon you and begin to torture you with the veriest inanities and absurdities ? Have you not felt that his chatterings were worse than the pain ? It must have been so with Jesus. When the ridiculous must needs question the sublime the result is misery. With the bloody sweat yet damp upon his brow, and with the accursed spittle still defacing his blessed countenance, the Man of Sorrows must be tortured by the drivellings of a heartless idler. With his heart all bowed down under a sense of the awful penalty of sin, the great Substitute for sinners must be molested by the petty small talk and ribald jests of the meanest of mankind. Solving eternal problems, and building up an everlasting temple unto the living God, he must be twitted by a vainglorious tetrarch, tormented and tortured by foolish questions fit only to be asked of a mountebank. We think the cross itself was not a worse instrument of torture than the haughty tongue of this debauched monarch.

Then the ribaldry of the whole thing must have tortured our Lord. The whole of them gathered round about him with their hoarse laughter and coarse jests. He has become a by-word and a proverb to them. When you are merry you can enjoy merriment ; but when the heart is sad laughter is wretchedly discordant, and embitters your grief. Now this one laughs, and then another sneers ; while a third thrusts out the tongue, and they are all uproariously jovial. In harmony they are all making nothing of him, though with awful earnestness he is lifting the world out of the slough of despair, and hanging it in its place again among the stars of glory. Jesus was performing more than Herculean labours, and these little beings, like so many gnats and flies, were stinging him. Small things are great at torturing, and these worthless beings did their utmost to torment our Lord. Oh, the torture of the Master's spirit !

Remember, it was no small sorrow to our Lord to be silent. You tell me that he appears majestic in his silence. It is even so ; but the pain of it was acute. Can you speak well ? Do you love to speak for the good of your fellow men, and do you know that when you speak full often your words are spirit and life to those who hear you ? It will be very hard to feel compelled to refuse them a good word. Do not imagine that the Lord despised Herod as Herod despised the Lord. Ah, no ! The pity of his soul went out to this poor frivolous creature who must needs make sport of the Saviour's sufferings, and treat the Son of the Highest as though he were a court fool, who must play before him. The Saviour's infinite love was breaking his heart ; for he longed to bless his persecutor, and yet he must not speak, nor give forth a warning word. True, there was little need for words, for his very presence was a sermon which ought to have melted a heart of stone ; but yet it cost the Saviour a mighty effort to keep down the flood-gates and hold in the blessed torrents of his holy speech, which would have flowed out in compassionate pleadings. Silent he must be ; but the anguish of it I can scarcely tell. Sometimes to be permitted to speak a word is the greatest comfort you can have. Have you never been in such a state that if you could cry out, it would have been a relief to you ? What anguish, then, to be forced to be as a dumb man ! What woe to be forced to be silent with all these mockers about him, and yet to be pitying them all ! As a man might pity a moth that flies into the flame of the candle, and will not be delivered, so did our Lord pity these creatures. How sad that they could make sport of their own damnation, fling the salvation of God to the ground, and tread it down as swine tread down their husks. Oh, it grieved the Master's heart ; it moved his soul to its very centre.

Think of the utter contempt that was poured upon him. I do not judge that this was the bitterest of his woes, for their contempt was an honour to him ; but yet it was one ingredient of his cup of mingled wormwood and gall, that they should so despise him as to clothe him in a white robe, and mock his kingship, when on that kingship their only hope was hung. They "set him at nought," that is, put him down as nothing, jeered and jested at him, and if there was nothing even about his manhood which they could respect, they invented ways by which they could pour scorn upon him. Luke is the gospel of the man ; if you want to read about Jesus in his manhood, read Luke ; and here you will see how his very manhood was trampled in the mire by these inhuman creatures, who found their joy in despising him.

See, then, your Lord and Master, and let me put two or three questions to you. Do you not think that this peculiar silence of Jesus was a part of his anguish, in which he was bearing the punishment for your sins of the tongue ? Ah me, ah me ! Redeemed of the Lord, how often have you misused your speech by wanton words ! How often have we uttered murmuring words, proud words, false words, words of despite to holy things ; and now our sins of the tongue are all coming upon him, and he must stand silent there and bear our penalty.

And is it not possible that when they put the gorgeous robe upon him, he was bearing your sins of vanity, your sins of dress and pride, when you made yourselves glorious to behold, and arrayed yourselves in gorgeous robes and glittering apparel ? Know ye not that these things are your shame ? For had you had no sin, you would have needed none of these poor rags ; and may not the Christ in white and red be bearing your sins of folly ? And do you not think that when they were making him nothing, and despising him, he was then bearing our sins, when we set him at nought—our words of despite and derision when, perhaps, in our ungodly days we, too, made sport of holy things, and jested at the word of God? Ah me, I think it was so, and I ask you to look at him, and say as you see him there, " It is not Herod after all; it is my tongue, my vanity, my trifling with holy things, which caused him this exquisite torture. Lord Jesus, substitute for me, let all these transgressions of mine be put away once for all by thy meritorious passion."

Finally, we read that Herod and Pilate were made friends from that day, and I do hope if there are any here that are true-hearted Christians if they have had any ill-will towards one another they will think it a great shame that Herod and Pilate should be friends, and that any two followers of Jesus should not be friends at the sight of the suffering Master. As for those two foxes, Pilate and Herod, they were tied tail to tail that day by our great Samson. Our Lord has often been a point of union for wicked men, not by his intent and purpose, but because they have joined together to oppose him. I have often smiled in my heart to see how superstition and scepticism will march together when they are anxious to oppose the gospel. Then the Sadducee says, " Give me your hand, dear Pharisee; we have a common interest here, for this man would overturn us all." The gospel is the mortal enemy both of the sceptical Sadducee and the superstitious Pharisee, and so they lay aside their differences to assail it. Now, then, if the wicked unite before our Lord Jesus when he wears the white robe, should not his people much more be united, especially when they remember that he said, " A new commandment give I unto you, that ye love one another." I charge you by your homage to him you call Master and Lord, if you have any difference of any sort with any Christian brother, let not yon sun go down till you have ended it by hearty love for Jesus' sake. Let it be seen that Christ is the great uniter of all those who are in him. He would have us love one another even as he has loved us, and his prayer is that we may be one. May the Lord hear that prayer, and make us one in Christ Jesus. Amen.

7. Inexcusable Irreverence and Ingratitude

"They are without excuse: because that, when they knew God, they glorified him not as God, neither were thankful."—Romans i. 20, 21.

THIS first chapter of the Epistle to the Romans is a dreadful portion of the Word of God. I should hardly like to read it all through aloud; it is not intended to be so used. Read it at home, and be startled at the awful vices of the Gentile world. Unmentionable crimes were the common pleasures of those wicked ages; but the chapter is also a striking picture of heathenism at the present time. After a missionary had gone into a certain part of Hindostan, and had given away New Testaments, a Hindoo waited upon him, and asked him this question: " Did you not write that first chapter in the Epistle to the Romans after you came here?" "No," replied the missionary, "I did not write it at all; it has been there nearly two thousand years." The Hindoo said, " Well, if it has not been written since you came here, all I can say is, that it might have been so written, for it is a fearfully true description of the sin of India." It is also much more true, even of London, than some of us would like to know. Even here are committed those vices, the very mention of which would make the cheek of modesty to crimson. However, I am not going to talk about Hindoos; they are a long way off. I am not going to speak about the ancient Romans; they lived a couple of thousand years ago. I am going to speak about ourselves, and about some persons here whom my text admirably fits. I fear that I am speaking to some who are " without excuse: because that, when they knew God, they glorified him not as God, neither were thankful."

I. The first charge against those who are mentioned in my text is, WANT OF REVERENCE. "They knew God," but "they glorified him not as God." They knew that there was a God; they never denied his existence; but they had no reverence for his name, they did not render to him the homage to which he is entitled, they did not glorify him as God.

Of many this is still true in this form, *they never think of God*. They go from year to year without any practical thought of God. Not only is he not in their words, but he is not in their thoughts. As the Psalmist puts it, "The wicked, through the pride of his countenance, will not seek after God: God is not in all his thoughts." The marginal reading is very expressive: "All his thoughts are, There is no God." Whether there is a God, or not, makes no practical difference to the wicked; they have so little esteem for him that, perhaps, if we could prove that there were no God, they would feel easier in their consciences. There must be something very wrong with you when you would rather that there were no God. "Well," says one, "I do not care much whether there is a God or not; I am an agnostic." Yes, a gentlemen once told me that he was an agnostic. "Oh!" I said, "that is a Greek word, is it not? And the equivalent Latin word is 'Ignoramus.'" Somehow, he did not like it in Latin nearly as well as in Greek. Oh, dear friends, I could not bear to be an "ignoramus" or an "agnostic" about God! I must have a God; I cannot do without him. He is to me as necessary as food to my body, and air to my lungs. The sad thing is, that many, who believe that there is a God, yet glorify him not as God, for they do not even give him a thought. I appeal to some here, whether this is not true. You go from the beginning of the week to the end of it without reflecting upon God at all. You could do as well without God as with him. Is not that the case? And must there not be something very terrible in the condition of your heart when, as a creature, you can do without a thought of your Creator, when he that has nourished you, and brought you up, is nothing to you, one of whom you never think?

These people, further, *have no right conceptions of God*. The true conception of God is that he is all in all. If God is anything, we ought to make him everything; you cannot put God in the second place. He is Almighty, All-wise, All-gracious, knowing everything, being in every place, constantly present, the emanations of his power found in every part of the universe. God is infinitely glorious; and unless we treat him as such, we have not treated him as he ought to be treated. If there be a king, and he is set to open the door or do menial work, he is not honoured as a king should be. Shall the great God be made a lackey to our lusts? Shall we put God aside, and say to him, "When I have a more convenient season, I will send for thee : when I have more money, I will attend to religion," or, "When I can be religious, and not lose anything by it, then I will seek thee"? Dost thou treat God so? Oh, beware, this is high treason against the King of kings! Wrong ideas of God, grovelling thoughts of God, come under the censure of the text, "When they knew God, they glorified him not as God."

Again, dear friends, there are some who think of God a little, but *they never offer him any humble, spiritual worship*. Do not imagine that God can be worshipped by anything which is merely mechanical or external, but which is not from the heart. A strange god must that god be who is pleased with what some men call worship. I have been into many a Romish church, and seen upon the altar paper flowers that would have been a disgrace to a tap-room; and I have said, "Is God pleased with this kind of thing?" Then I have been into a better building, and I have seen crucifixes and altars adorned like a fine lapidary's shop; and I have said to myself, "They might adorn a bride; but God cares not for jewels." Is your conception of God that he desires your gold and your silver, and your brass and your fine linen, and all these adornments? Thou thinkest that he is such an one as thyself. Surely, thou hast poor conceptions of God. When the organ peals out its melodious tones, but the heart is not in the singing, dost thou think that God has ears like those of a man, that can be tickled with sweet sounds? Why hast thou brought him down to thy level? He is spiritual; the music that delights him is the love of a true heart, the prayer of an anxious spirit. He has better music than all your organs and drums can ever bring to him. If he wanted music, he would not have asked thee, for winds and waves make melodies transcendently superior to all that your chief musicians can compose. Does he want candles when his touch makes the mountains to be great altars, smoking with the incense of praise to the God of creation? Oh, brethren, I fear that it has been true of many who externally appeared to be devout, "when they knew God, they glorified him not as God"! Weep over your sin: now have you glorified him as God. Fall on your face, and be nothing before the Most High: now have you glorified him as God. Accept his righteousness; adore his bleeding Son; trust in his infinite compassion. Now have you glorified him as God, for "God is a Spirit, and they that worship him must worship him in spirit and in truth." How far, my dear hearers, have you complied with that requisition?

Further, the people mentioned in my text did not glorify God, *for they did not obediently serve him.* My dear hearer, have *you* served God? Have you looked upon yourself as a servant of God? When you awoke in the morning, did you say, "What does God expect me to do to-day?" When you have summed up the day, have you applied this test, "How far have I endeavoured to serve God to-day?" There are many who are the servants of themselves; and there is no master more tyrannical than unsanctified self. Many are toiling, like slaves at the galleys, for wealth, for honour, for respectability, for something for themselves. But, remember, if the Lord be God, and he made us, we are bound to serve him. How is it that God has kept you alive these forty years, perhaps twice forty, and yet you have never glorified him as God, by rendering him any service whatsoever? This is a very solemn enquiry. I should like everyone whom it concerns to take it home to his own conscience.

There is another charge to be brought against those who glorified not God, although they knew him; that is, *they did not trust him.* The place for man is under the shadow of God's wings. If he made me, I ought to seek him in the hour of trouble. In the time of my need I should apply to his bounty. If I feel unhappy, I should look to him for comfort. My dear hearers, are there not some of you who never did trust God yet? You run to your neighbours as soon as ever you are in difficulties. You trust your old uncle; but you never trust your God. Oh, what a wretched business is this, if God, who is all truth and all love, does not have the confidence of his own creatures! Remember how the Lord spake by the mouth of Jeremiah: "Cursed be the man that trusteth in man, and maketh flesh his arm, and whose heart departeth from the Lord. For he shall be like the heath in the desert, and shall not see when good cometh; but shall inhabit the parched places in the wilderness, in a salt land and not inhabited. Blessed is the man that trusteth in the Lord, and whose hope the Lord is. For he shall be as a tree planted by the waters, and that spreadeth out her roots by the river, and shall not see when heat cometh, but her leaf shall be green; and shall not be careful in the year of drought, neither shall cease from yielding fruit." The people mentioned in the text knew God, but they did not trust him.

In addition to this, *they did not seek to commune with him.* Are there not some here who never tried to speak to God? It never occurred to you, did it? And God has not spoken to you; at least, you have not known whose voice it was when he did speak. It is a very sad business when a boy, who has been at home with his father and mother for years, has never spoken to them. He came down in the morning, and ate his breakfast; he came in, and devoured his dinner; he took his supper with them night by night; but he never spoke to them. Would you have a boy of that kind living with you? You would be obliged to say, "John, you must go; it pains me to send you away, but I cannot bear to have you sitting here in silence. If I speak to you, you never answer me." Some of you cannot remember the time when you spoke to God, or God spoke to you; it is so very long ago, if it ever did occur in your past experience. There is a man somewhere here who did speak to God the other day. He called upon God with a foul and blasphemous oath. When he was telling a lie, he called upon God to witness to it. Ah! yes, you have broken the silence; but it would have been better not to have spoken, than to have uttered those vile blasphemies against the Most High. Your horrible words have entered into the ears of the Lord God of Sabaoth; and, as the Lord liveth, you will have to answer for them to the great Judge of all men, unless you seek his face, and find forgiveness through his Son. Our Saviour said that, for every *idle* word that men shall speak, they shall give account in the day of judgment; how much more shall they be required to answer for every evil, false, slanderous, blasphemous word they have spoken!

But are there not many persons who have never uttered an oath, and are scrupulously careful about speaking the truth, who have never had any spiritual converse with God? Wretched creatures indeed are you; even though you are wealthy and prosperous, you have missed the highest good, the best blessing that man can know.

There are some who, although they know God, do not glorify him, because, while conscious of their enmity against God, *they do not want to be reconciled to him.* There is a way of perfect reconciliation between God and man. Whosoever believeth in Christ Jesus is at once forgiven; he is adopted into the family of God; he drinks of the wine of the love of God; he is saved with an everlasting salvation. There are many who know this in their minds; but it never excites any desire for it in their hearts. No, whether reconciled or unreconciled, does not trouble them. Knowest thou, O man, that the English of it is, "I defy God; I neither want his love, nor fear his hate; I will lift my face before his thunderbolts, and dare him to do his worst"? Oh, fatal defiance of the blessed God! May the Spirit of God work upon thy conscience now, to make thee see the evil of this condition, and turn from it! While I speak, I feel deeply troubled to have to say what I do; but I am only speaking of what many a conscience here must confess to be true. You live, some of you, knowing God, but not glorifying him as God.

II. Now I take from my text the second accusation, which is certainly quite as sad as the other. Those who are mentioned by Paul are accused of WANT OF GRATITUDE. It is said of them that "when they knew God, they glorified him not as God, neither were thankful."

I cannot say anything much worse of a man than that he is not thankful to those who have been his benefactors; and when you say that he is not thankful to God, you have said about the worst thing you can say of him. Now look not merely at the people who lived in Paul's day, but at those who are living now. I will soon prove ingratitude on the part of many. There are many counts in the indictment we have to bring against them in God's High Court of Justice.

First, *God's law is despised.* You young men and women, who are beginning life, if you are intelligent and wise, say, "We wish that we knew what we ought to do for our own preservation and happiness; and we should also like to know what to avoid lest we should do ourselves harm." Well, now, the book of the law of the ten commands is simply the sanitary regulation of the moral world, telling us what would damage us, and what would benefit us. We ought to be very thankful to have such plain directions. "Thou shalt." "Thou shalt not." But see. God has taken the trouble to give us this map of the way, and to direct us in the only right road; yet some have despised the heavenly guide. They have gone directly in the teeth of that law; in fact, it looks as if the very existence of the law has been a provocation to them to break it. Is not this a piece of dreadful ingratitude? Whenever God says, "Thou shalt not," it is because it would be mischievous to us to do it. Sometimes, in London, when the ice in the parks is not strong enough to bear, they put up boards on which is the word "Dangerous." Who but a fool would go where that danger-signal is? The ten commands indicate what is dangerous: nay, what is fatal. Keep clear of all that is forbidden.

Next, *God's day is dishonoured* by those who are not thankful to him. God has, in great mercy, given us a day, one day in seven, wherein to rest, and to think of holy things. There were seven days that God had in the week. He said, "Take six, and use them in your business." No, we must have the seventh as well. It is as if one, upon the road, saw a poor man in distress, and having but seven shillings, the generous person gave the poor man six; but when the wretch had scrambled on his feet, he followed his benefactor to knock him down,

and steal the seventh shilling from him. How many do this! The
Sabbath is their day for sport, for amusement, for anything but the
service of God. They rob God of his day, though it be but one in
seven. This is base unthankfulness. May not many here confess
that they have been guilty of it? If so, let no more Sabbaths be
wasted; but let their sacred hours, and all the week between, be spent
in diligent search after God; and then, when you have found him, the
Lord's-day will be the brightest gem of all the seven, and you will
sing with Dr. Watts,—

> " Welcome, sweet day of rest,
>   That saw the Lord arise ;
>   Welcome to this reviving breast,
>   And these rejoicing eyes ! "

Moreover, *God's Book is neglected* by these ungrateful beings. He
has given us a Book; here is a copy of it. Was there ever such a
Book, so full of wisdom, and so full of love ? Let a man look at it
on bended knee; for he may find heaven between these pages. But,
when God has taken the trouble to make this wonderful Book, there
are many who do not take the trouble to read it. Ah, me, what
ingratitude ! A father's love-letter to his son, and his son leaves it
unread ! Here is a Book, the like of which is not beneath the cope of
heaven, and God has exercised even his omniscience to make it a
perfect Book, for all ranks and conditions of men, in all periods of
the world's history; and yet, such is man's ingratitude, that he turns
away from it.

But there is something much worse ; *God's Son is refused* by the
unthankful. God had but one Son, and such a Son; one with himself, infinite, holy, his delight ! He took him from his bosom, and
sent him to this earth. The Son took our nature, and became a
servant, and then died the death of a felon, the death of the cross,
and all to save us, all for the guilty, all for men who were his
enemies. I feel guilty myself while I am talking about it, that I do
not burst into tears. This must be one of the mysteries that angels
cannot comprehend, that after Christ had died, there were found
sinners who would not be saved by him. They refused to be washed
in the fountain filled with blood; they rejected eternal life, even
though it streamed from the five great founts of his wounded body.
They chose hell rather than salvation by his blood. They were so in
love with their dire enemy, sin, that they would not be reconciled to
God even by the death of his Son. Oh, ingratitude, thou hast reached
thy utmost limit now, for thou hast trodden under foot the Son of
God, and hast counted the blood of the covenant, wherewith he was
sanctified, an unholy thing, and hast done despite unto the Spirit of
grace ! Is not this terrible ?

I might stop here; but, for the sake of pricking the consciences of
some, I want to say, dear friends, that there are some persons so
ungrateful, that *God's deliverances are forgotten.* Some years ago, I
spoke with a soldier who rode in the fatal charge at Balaclava ; and
when he told me so, I took him by the hand; I could not help it,
though he was a stranger to me. The tears were in my eyes, and I

said, " Sir, I hope that you are God's man after such a deliverance as that." Almost all the saddles emptied, shot and shell flying to the right and left, death mowing down the whole brigade ; yet he escaped. But I did not find that he had given his heart to Christ. Over there is a man who has been in half-a-dozen shipwrecks ; and if he does not mind, he will be shipwrecked to all eternity! One here has had yellow fever. Ah, sir, there is a worse fever than that on you now ! I cannot speak of all the cases here of strange deliverances ; but I do not doubt that I address some who have been between the jaws of death. They have looked over the edge of that dread precipice, beneath which is the fathomless abyss. You vowed that, if God would spare your life, you would never be what you were before ; and in truth you are not, for you are worse than ever. You are sinning now against light, and in shameful ingratitude. God have mercy upon you !

How often, dear friends, is there ingratitude on the part of uncon-verted men in the matter of *God's providences ignored !* Why, look at some of you ! You never missed a meal in your lives. When you went to the table, there was always something on it. You never had to lose a night's rest for want of a bed. Some of you, from your childhood, have had all that heart could wish. If God has treated you so, while many are crushed with poverty, should he not have some gratitude from you? You had a good mother ; you had a tender father ; you have gone from one form of relationship to another with increasing comfort. You are spared, and your mother is spared ; your wife and children are spared. Indeed, God has made your path very smooth. Some of you are getting on in business, while other men are failing ; some of you have every comfort at home, while others have been widowed, and their children have fallen one after the other. Will you never be grateful? Hard, hard heart, wilt thou never break ? Will any mercy bend thee ? Must there be a storm of wrath to break thee in pieces, like a potter's vessel ? Will not love and tenderness melt thee ? I do appeal to some here, whose path has been so full of mercies, that they ought to think of God, and turn to him with sincere repentance and faith.

But one says, " I have had good luck." What can be worse than that ? Here is unthankfulness to God indeed, when you ascribe his good gifts to " good luck." " Well, you know, but I have been a very hard-working man." I know you have, but who gave you the strength for your work ? " I have had a good supply of brains while others have not." Did you make your own brains ? Do you not feel that any man who talks about his own wisdom, and his own wit, writes " FOOL " across his forehead in capital letters ? We owe every-thing to God ; shall we give God nothing ? Shall we have no gratitude to him from whom all our blessings have come ? God forgive us if it has been so, and give us grace to alter our past course at once !

Once more, there is another piece of ingratitude of which many are guilty, *God's Spirit is resisted by them.* The Spirit of God comes to them, and gently touches them. Perhaps he has done so to-night while you have been sitting here. You have said, " Do not talk quite so plainly to us. Give us a little comfort, a little breathing space ; and do not be quite so hard on us." I hope that it was the Spirit of God rather than the preacher who was dealing with you. At any rate, he has done so a good many times; and you have tried to drive from your heart your best Friend. You have been so ungenerous to him that, when he came to lead you to Christ, you summoned all your strength, and the devil came to help you, and up till now you have resisted the Spirit of God with some degree of success. The Lord have mercy upon you! But how true is my text still, even of many who are found in the house of prayer, "When they knew God, they glorified him not as God, neither were thankful"!

III. Now I finish with my third point, which is, that THIS IRRE-VERENCE AND INGRATITUDE WERE AGAINST KNOWLEDGE. "When they knew God, they glorified him not as God, neither were thankful."

Will you kindly notice, that, according to my text, *knowledge is of no use if it does not lead to holy practice?* "They knew God." It was no good to them to know God, for "they glorified him not as God." So my theological friend over there, who knows so much that he can split hairs over doctrines, it does not matter what you think, or what you know, unless it leads you to glorify God, and to be thankful. Nay, your knowledge may be a millstone about your neck to sink you down in woe eternal, unless your knowledge is turned to holy practice.

Indeed, *knowledge will increase the responsibility of those who are irreverent and ungrateful.* Paul says, "They are without excuse: because that, when they knew God, they glorified him not as God, neither were thankful." Whatever excuse might be made for those who never heard of God, there was none for these people. My dear hearers, you also are "without excuse." Many of you have had godly parents, you have attended a gospel ministry, your Sunday-school teachers and Christian friends have taught you the way of salvation; you are not ignorant. If you do not glorify God, if you are not thankful to him, it will be more tolerable for the people of Sodom and Gomorrah at the day of judgment than for you, for they never had the privileges that you have despised. Remember how the Saviour upbraided the cities wherein most of his mighty works were done, because they repented not: "Woe unto thee, Chorazin! Woe unto thee, Bethsaida! for if the mighty works, which were done in you, had been done in Tyre and Sidon, they would have repented long ago in sackcloth and ashes." I hardly know which is the greater wonder, that the people who saw Christ's mighty works did not repent, or that those who would have repented if they had seen those works were not permitted to see them.

I wish, dear friends, that you could get out of this state of not glorify-ing God, and not being thankful. Surely, you only want to have the case stated, and the Spirit of God to speak to your conscience, to cause you to say, "I cannot bear to be in such a dreadful condition with regard to God any longer." May God enable you to repent to-night! Change your mind. That is the meaning of the word "repent." Change your mind, and say, "We will glorify God. There is a Great First Cause. There is a Creator. There must be an omnipotent, all-wise Being. We will worship him. We will say in our hearts, 'This God shall be our God, and we will trust him if he will but accept us.'"

Then remember the years that are past. They involve a great debt, and you cannot pay it; for, if you go on serving God without a flaw till the end of your life, there is the old debt still due; there are the years that are gone, and "God requireth the years that are past." Well, now, hear what he has done. He has given his dear Son to "bear our sins in his own body on the tree"; and, if you will trust Christ, then know of a surety that Christ has put away your sin, and you are forgiven. "Look,"—that is his word—"Look unto me, and be ye saved, all ye ends of the earth." When the brazen serpent was lifted up, all that those who were bitten had to do was to look at the serpent of brass; and everyone that looked, lived. If any man of that crowd had looked at Moses, that would not have healed him. If he had looked at the fiery serpents, and tried to pull them off, that would not have healed him. But he looked to the brazen serpent, and, as his eyes caught the gleam of the brass, the deadly serpent's bites were healed, and the man lived. Look to Jesus. Look now. May God the Holy Spirit lead you to do so!

"I do not feel fit," says one. That is looking to yourself. "I do not feel my need enough," says another. That is trusting to your sense of need. Away with everything that is in you, or about you, and just trust Christ, and you shall immediately be saved. Whoever, in this great congregation, will but look to Jesus, shall be saved upon the spot. However great your iniquities, however stony your heart, however despairing your mind, look, look, look, look. And then, when you look to Christ, your ingratitude will be forgiven, and it will die. You will love him who has loved you, and you shall be saved, and saved for ever.

When we received eighty-two into the church last Lord's-day evening, I could not help breathing an earnest prayer that this might be the beginning of a revival. May it come to-night, and may many in these two galleries, and down below, be carried away by that blessed tide of mighty grace that shall sweep them off their feet, and land them safe on the Rock of ages!

Will you, dear friends, pray for this? I shall feel that even my poor, weak instrumentality will be quite sufficient for the greatest work if I have your prayers at my back. Will you to-night, at the family altar, or at your own bedsides, make it a special subject of prayer that men, who knew God, but glorified him not as God, and were not thankful, may to-night turn to God? If I could get at some of you who are living without Christ, I should like to do what the Roman ambassadors used to do. When they came to a king who was at war with the empire, they said to him, "Will you have peace with Rome, or not?" If he said that he must have time to think it over, the ambassador, with his rod, drew a ring round the man, and said, "You must decide before you cross that line, for, if you do not say 'Peace' before you step out of it, Rome will crush you with her armies." There are no doors to the pews, else I would say, "Shut those doors, and do not let the people out until God decides them." Lord, shut them in! Lord, arrest them: hold them fast, and let them not go till each one of them has said, "I believe; help thou mine unbelief." May God bless you all, for Jesus' sake! Amen.

8. "Marvelous Things"

"O sing unto the LORD a new song; for he hath done marvellous things: his right hand, and his holy arm, hath gotten him the victory. The LORD hath made known his salvation: his righteousness hath he openly shewed in the sight of the heathen."—Psalm xcviii. 1, 2.

THE invitations of the gospel are invitations to happiness. In delivering God's message, we do not ask men to come to a funeral, but to a wedding feast. If our errand were one of sorrow, we might not marvel if men refused to listen to us; but it is one of gladness, not sadness—in fact, you might condense the gospel message into this joyous invitation, "O come, and learn how to sing unto the Lord a new song! Come and find peace, rest, joy, and all else that your souls can desire. Come and eat ye that which is good, and let your soul delight itself in fatness." When the coming of Christ to the earth was first announced, it was not with sad sonorous sounds of devil spirits driven from the nethermost hell, but with the choral symphonies of holy angels who joyfully sang, "Glory to God in the highest, and on earth peace, good will toward men;" and as long as ever the gospel shall be preached in this world, its main message will be one of joy. The gospel is a source of joy to those who proclaim it, for unto us, who are less than the least of all saints, is this grace given—that we should preach among the Gentiles the unsearchable riches of Christ. The gospel is also a source of joy to all who hear it aright, and accept it, for its very name means "glad tidings of good things." I feel that, if I am not able to preach to you as I would, yet am I thrice happy in being permitted to preach at all; and if the style and manner of my address may not be such as I desire them to be, nor such as you will commend, yet it will matter but little, for the simplest telling out of the gospel is of itself a most delightful thing; and if our hearts were in a right condition, we should not merely be glad to hear of Jesus over and over again, but the story of the love of our Incarnate God, and of the redemption wrought by Immanuel, would be the sweetest music that our ears ever heard.

In the hope that our hearts may thus rejoice, I am going to talk of many things under two heads. The first is, *the marvellous things which God has done in the person of his Son;* and, secondly, *some marvellous things in reference to ourselves,* which are almost as marvellous as those that God has done.

I. Firstly, I am to call your attention to THE MARVELLOUS THINGS MENTIONED IN THE TEXT. If you read it carefully, you will notice that, first, there are some marvellous things that are marvellous in themselves; secondly, some that were marvellous in the way in which they were done: "His right hand, and his holy arm, hath gotten him the victory;" and then, thirdly, some that were marvellous as to the way in which they were made known: "The Lord hath made known his salvation: his righteousness hath he openly shewed in the sight of the heathen."

First, then, we will consider *the things that are marvellous in themselves:* "He hath done marvellous things: his right hand, and his holy arm, hath gotten him the victory." You know the story. We were enslaved by sin, we were in such bondage that we were liable to be for ever in chains; but our great Champion undertook our cause, and entered the lists pledged to fight for us till the end; and he has done it. It would have been a cause of great joy if I could have come here, and said to you, "The Lord Jesus Christ has undertaken to fight our battles for us;" but I have something much better than that to say. He has fought the fight, and "his holy arm hath gotten him the victory." It must have required more faith to believe in the Christ who was to come than to believe in the Christ who has come. It must have required no little faith to believe in Christ as victorious while he was in the midst of the struggle; for instance, when the bloody sweat was falling amidst the olive trees, or when he was hanging upon the cross, and moaning out that awful cry, "My God, my God, why hast thou forsaken me?" But the great crisis is past. No longer does the issue of the conflict tremble in the balance; Christ hath for ever accomplished his warfare, and our foes are all beneath his feet.

> "Love's redeeming work is done;
> Fought the fight, the battle won."

What foes has Christ overcome? Our main foe, our sin, both as to the guilt of it and as to the power of it. As to the guilt of it, there was a law, which we had broken, and which must be satisfied. Christ has kept the positive precepts of that law in his own perfect life, and he has vindicated the honour of that law by his sacrificial death upon the cross. The law, therefore, being satisfied, the strength of sin is gone; and now, O believers, the sins which ye saw in the day of your conviction ye shall see no more for ever! As Moses triumphantly sang of the enemies of the chosen people, "the depths have covered them," so can you say of your sins, "There is not one of them left." Even in God's great

Book of Remembrance there is no record of sin against any believer in the Lord Jesus Christ. "By him all that believe are justified from all things." Try to realize this, brethren and sisters in Christ. Let the great army of your sins pass before you in review, —each one like a son of Anak, armed to the teeth for your destruction. They have gone down into the depths, and the Red Sea of Christ's blood has drowned them, and so he hath gained a complete victory over all the guilt of sin; and as for the power of sin within us,—alas! we often groan concerning it, but let us groan no longer; or if we do, let us also sing.

The experience of a Christian is summed up in Paul's utterance, "O wretched man that I am! who shall deliver me from the body of this death? I thank God through Jesus Christ our Lord."* If you take the whole quotation, I believe you have a summary of a spiritual man's life,—a daily groaning and a daily boasting,—a daily humbling and a daily rejoicing,—a daily consciousness of sin and a daily consciousness of the power of the Lord Jesus Christ to conquer it. We do believe, beloved, that our sin has received its death-blow. It still lingers within us, for its death is by crucifixion, and crucifixion is a lingering death. Its heart is not altogether fastened to the cross, but its hands are, so that we cannot sin as we once did. Its feet, too, are fastened, so that we cannot run in the way of transgressors as we once did; and one of these days the spear shall pierce its heart, and it shall utterly die; and, then, with the faultless ones before the throne of God, we shall be unattended by depravity or corruption any longer. Therefore, let us "sing unto the Lord a new song," because his right hand, and his holy arm, have gotten him the victory over sin within us.

> "His be the victor's name,
>   Who fought our fight alone;
> Triumphant saints no honour claim;
>   His conquest was his own."

In connection with sin came death, for death is the daughter of sin, and follows closely upon sin; Jesus has conquered death. It is not possible for believers to die eternally, for Jesus said, "Because I live, ye shall live also;" and even the character of the natural death is changed to believers. It is not now a penal infliction, but a necessary way of elevating our nature from the bondage of corruption into the glorious liberty of the children of God, for "flesh and blood cannot inherit the kingdom of God." Even those who will be living at the coming of the Lord must be "changed" in order that they may be fit to enter glory. Death, therefore, to believers, is but a putting off of our week-day garments that we may put on our Sabbatic attire,—the laying aside of the travel-stained garments of earth that we may put on the pure vestments of joy for ever. So we do not fear death now, for Christ has conquered it. He has rent away the iron bars of the grave, and he has left in the sepulchre his own winding-sheets and

*See *The New Park Street Pulpit*, No. 235, "The Fainting Warrior."

napkin that there may be suitable furniture in what was once a grim, cold, empty charnel-house; and he has gone up into his glory, and left heaven's gate wide open to all believers. Unless he shall first come, we too shall descend into the grave whither he went, but we also shall come up again as he did, and we shall rise complete in the perfection of our redeemed manhood. Then shall we be satisfied, when we awake in the likeness of our Master; so let us "sing unto the Lord a new song, for he hath done marvellous things."

> "Hosannah to the Prince of light,
>   Who clothed himself in clay,
>   Enter'd the iron gates of death,
>   And tore the bars away!
>
> "Death is no more the king of dread,
>   Since our Immanuel rose;
>   He took the tyrant's sting away,
>   And spoil'd our hellish foes.
>
> "See how the Conqueror mounts aloft,
>   And to his Father flies,
>   With scars of honour in his fleh,
>   And triumph in his eyes"

And as Christ has conquered sin and death, so has he conquered the devil and all his hosts of fallen spirits. This monster of iniquity, this monster of craft and malice has striven to hold us in perpetual bondage; but Christ met him in the wilderness, and vanquished him there; and met him, as I believe, in the garden of Gethsemane, in personal conflict, and vanquished him once for all; and now he has led captivity captive. Inferior spirits were driven away by Christ when he was here upon earth, and they fled at the bidding of the King; and now, although Satan still worries and vexes the saints of God, the Lord will bruise Satan under their feet shortly. Therefore, dear brethren and sisters in Christ, this is the joyous news we have to bring to sinners,—that sin, and death, and the devil have all been vanquished by the great Captain of our salvation; and for this let us so rejoice that we sing unto the Lord a new song.

> "He hell in hell laid low;
>   Made sin, he sin o'erthrew:
>   Bow'd to the grave, destroy'd it so,
>   And death, by dying slew.
>
> "Sin, Satan, death appear
>   To harass and appal;
>   Yet since the gracious Lord is near,
>   Backward they go, and fall."

But, according to the text, what the Lord did is not only marvellous in itself, but *the way in which he did it was also marvellous.* Observe that he did it alone: "His own right hand, and his holy arm, hath gotten him the victory." No one was associated with the Lord Jesus Christ in the conquest which he achieved over sin, and death, and the devil, and nothing is more abhorrent to a believing soul than the idea of giving any particle of glory to anyone but the Lord Jesus Christ. He trod the winepress alone, so let him alone wear the crown. Sinner, you have not to look for any secondary Saviour; Christ has done it all. You need pay no reverence to saints, or martyrs, or priests Christ has done it all, so resort, to him for all you want. Christ alone has accomplished the salvation of his people; no other hand has been raised to help him in the fight. Look then to Jesus only for salvation. Trust in him with your whole heart; throw your weight entirely upon him, my poor brother or sister, if you have not yet done so, and you shall find rest and salvation in him.

Another marvel is that he did it all so wisely: "His right hand hath gotten him the victory." You know that we use the word "dexterous" to signify a thing that is done well; we mean that it was done right-handedly. So Christ fought our battle with his right hand; he did it with ease, with strength, and with infinite wisdom. Salvation is the very perfection of wisdom, because, in the salvation of a sinner, all the attributes of God are equally glorified. There is as much justice as there is mercy in the salvation of a sinner by the atoning sacrifice of Christ,—mercy full-orbed, and justice full-orbed also,—God fulfilling his threatenings against sin by smiting Christ, and giving to the love of his heart full vent in saving the very chief of sinners through the death of his dear Son. The more I consider the doctrine of substitution, the more is my soul enamoured of the matchless wisdom of God which devised this system of salvation. As for a hazy atonement which atones for everybody in general, and for nobody in particular,— an atonement made equally for Judas and for John, I care nothing for it; but a literal, substitutionary sacrifice, Christ vicariously bearing the wrath of God on my behalf, this calms my conscience with regard to the righteous demands of the law of God, and satisfies the instincts of my nature which declare that, as God is just, he must exact the penalty of my guilt. Dear brethren, Jesus Christ, suffering, bleeding, dying, has gotten us the victory. The hand that was pierced by the nails has conquered sin, the hand that was fastened to the wood has fastened up the accusation that was written against us, the hand that bled has brought salvation to us, so that we are Christ's for ever. 'Twas infinite wisdom which shone in the conquest of sin, and death, and the devil.

But it was holiness too: "His holy arm hath gotten him the victory." The psalmist seems, as he advances in his Psalms, to fall more and more in love with the matchless holiness of God, and the holiness of the victory of Christ is a great point in its favour. There is never a sinner so saved as to make God even seem to wink at sin. Since the creation of this world, there was never an act of mercy performed by God that was not in perfect harmony with the severest justice. God, though he has loved and saved unholy men, has never stained his holy hands in the act of saving them. He still remains the holy, holy, holy, Lord God of Sabaoth, though he is still very pitiful, and full of compassion, and passes by transgression, iniquity, and sin, and presses prodigal children to his heart. The atonement of Jesus Christ is the answer to the great question, "How can God be just and yet the Justifier of him that believeth? How can he be perfectly holy, and yet, at the same time, receive into his love, and adopt into his family, those who are unrighteous and unholy?" O Calvary, thou hast solved he problem! The bleeding wounds of the Incarnate God have made righteousness and peace to kiss each other. May God grant to you, unconverted sinner, the grace to understand how he can save you, and yet be perfectly holy, how he can forgive your sins, and yet be perfectly just! I know this is the difficulty that troubles you,—how can you be received while God is what he is? He can receive you, for the Lord Jesus Christ took the sin of his people, and bore it in his own body on the tree, and being the appointed Head of all believers, he has vindicated in his own person the inflexible justice of God. There is the Man who has kept the whole law of God,—not Adam, for he failed to keep it,— but the second Adam, the Lord from heaven; and all whom he represented are now "accepted in the Beloved," made acceptable to God because of what Jesus Christ has done. So let us magnify that holy arm which hath gotten him the victory.

I have now to speak upon the third point, *the marvellous grace which has revealed all this to us.* It is a very familiar thing for us who are sitting here to hear the gospel, but will you just carry your minds back, some two or three thousand years, to the period when this Psalm was written? What was then known concerning salvation was known almost exclusively by the Jews. Here and there, a proselyte was led into the bonds of the covenant; but, for the most part, the whole world lay in heathen darkness. Where there was the seal of circumcision, there were the oracles of God; but as for the sinners of the Gentiles, they knew nothing whatever concerning the truth. And it might have been so till this day if the Lord had not made known his salvation, and openly showed his righteousness in the sight of the heathen. Our present privileges are greater than those of ancient Israel, and I am afraid that we sometimes despise or at least forget, those whom we have for a time supplanted. They were the favoured people of God, and through their unbelief they have been put away for a while, but Israel is yet to be restored to even greater blessings than it formerly enjoyed.

> "The hymn shall yet in Zion swell
> That sounds Messiah's praise,
> And thy loved name, Immanuel!
> As once in ancient days.
>
> " F r Israel yet shall own her King,
> For her salvation waits,
> And hill and dale shall sweetly sing
> With praise in all her gates."

Do we value as we ought the privilege we now have of hearing in our own tongue the wonderful works of God? My dear unconverted hearer, how grateful you ought to be that you were not born in Rome, or Babylon, or in the far-off Indies, in those days when there was no Christian missionary to seek you out, and care for your soul, but when the whole of the light that shone was shed upon that little land of Palestine! Jesus Christ has broken down the middle wall of partition, and now it makes no difference whether we are Barbarian, Scythian, bond or free, for the gospel is to be preached to every creature in all the world, and "he that believeth and is baptized shall be saved," whatever his previous character may have been, or to whatever race he may have belonged.

Yet let us never forget that, in order to accomplish this great work of salvation, it was necessary that the blessed Son of God should descend to this world, and it was also necessary that the Spirit of God should be given to rest upon the Church, to be the inspiration by which the gospel should be preached among the heathen. Again let me ask a question. Do we sufficiently reverence the Holy Ghost, and love him as we should for all that he has done? The incarnation of the Son of God is no greater mystery than the indwelling of the Spirit of God in the hearts of men. It is truly marvellous that the ever-blessed Spirit, who is equally God with the Father and the Son, should come and reside in these bodies of ours, and make them his temple. Yet remember that, if it had not been so, there would have been no effective preaching of the gospel; and, this night, unless the Holy Ghost is here to bless the Word, there will be no open showing of Christ's righteousness to you, and no making known of his salvation to your heart. All the victories of Christ, for which I challenge your grateful songs, would be unknown to you if the Holy Ghost did not touch men's lips so that they might tell what the Lord hath done, and publish abroad his glorious victories.

Remember, too, that, in connection with the work of the Holy Spirit, there has had to be an unbroken chain of divine providence to bring the gospel to you, and to your fellow-countrymen. Look back through the past ages, and see what wonderful revolutions of the wheels full of eyes there have been. Empires have risen, and have fallen, but their rise and fall have had a close connection with the preaching of the gospel. There have been terrific persecutions of the saints of God; Satan has seemed to summon all hell to attack the Church of Christ, yet he could not destroy its life. Then came the night of Popery, dense as the nights of Egypt's darkness; but old Rome could not put out the light of the gospel. Since then, in what marvellous ways has God led his chosen people! He has raised up his servants, one after another, so that the testimony concerning the victories achieved by Christ might be continued among us, and might be spread throughout all the nations of the earth; and thus it comes to pass that, to-night, you have the open Bible in your hands, and I am permitted freely to expound the teaching of that Bible to you. How wonderfully has the history of our own country been working towards this happy result! Glorify God and bless his holy name that we live in such halcyon days as these when the Lord hath made known his salvation, and hath openly showed his righteousness in the sight of the heathen.

But yet more sweetly let us praise the Lord that we not only live where the gospel is made known, but that God has made it known to some of us in a still higher sense. Some of us now understand, as we did not at one time, the righteousness of God,—his way of making men righteous through Jesus Christ. We understood it in theory long before God made it savingly known in our soul; this is another work of the Holy Spirit for which we have good reason to sing unto the Lord a new song. Sinner, I have to say to you that God has sent the gospel to you to tell you that his Son, Jesus Christ, has conquered sin, and death, and the devil, and that, if you believe in Jesus, you shall be a partaker in his victory. There is nothing for you to do but to believe in him. Even the power to understand his truth is God's gift to you; even the faith that receives it he works in you according to his Spirit. You are to be nothing that God may be everything; it is for you to fall at his feet, with confusion of face and contrition of heart, and when he bids you do so, to rise up and say, "I will sing unto the Lord a new song. O Lord, I will praise thee; for though thou wast angry with me, thine anger is turned away, and thou comfortedst me through him who hath gotten the victory on my behalf."

II. The second point of my subject, on which I must speak very briefly indeed, is this,—THERE ARE SOME MARVELLOUS THINGS IN REFERENCE TO OURSELVES.

The first of these marvellous things is that, after all that Christ has done, and the mercy of God in making it known, *so many are utterly careless and indifferent concerning it.* Tens of thousands will not even cross the threshold to go and hear about it. Bibles are in many of their houses, yet they do not take the trouble to read them. If they are going on a railway journey, they consult their *Bradshaw;* but they do not search God's own Guide Book to find the way to heaven, or to learn where and when they must start if they mean to reach that place of eternal happiness and bliss. We can still ask, with Isaiah, "Who hath believed our report? and to whom is the arm of the Lord revealed?" The most marvellous sight out of hell is an unconverted man; it is a marvel of marvels that the Son of God himself should leave heaven and all its glories, and come to earth to bleed and die, in manhood's shape for manhood's sake, and yet that there should be anyone in the shape of a man who should not care even to hear the story of his wondrous sacrifice, or that hearing the story, should disregard it as if it were of no interest to him. Yet see how men rush to buy a newspaper when there is some little bit of news! With what avidity do some young people, and some old people too, who ought to know better, read the foolish story of a love-sick maid! How freely their tears flow over imaginary griefs! Yet the Lord Jesus

Christ, bleeding to death in disinterested love to his enemies, moves them not to tears, and their hearts remain untouched by the story of his sufferings as if they were made of marble.

The depravity of mankind is a miracle of sin; it is as great a miracle, from one point of view, as the grace of God is from another. Jesus Christ neglected! Eternal love slighted! Infinite mercy disregarded! Ay, and I have to confess, with great shame, that even the preacher of the gospel is not always affected by it as he ought to be; and not only must I, my brethren, confess this, but so must others, I fear, who preach the Word. Why, it ought to make us dance for joy to have to tell you that there is mercy in the heart of God, that there is pardon for sinners, that there is life for the dead, that the great heart of God yearns over sinners; and our hearts ought to be ready to break when we find that men disregard all this good news, and are not affected by it. It is an astounding calamity that men should have fallen so terribly that they are insensible to infinite love. God grant that his grace may show to you, unconverted sinners here, in what a horrible state your hearts must be in that, after all that Christ has done, you still give him no token of gratitude, no song of praise for the wonders he has wrought.

Looking from this point of view, there is another marvellous thing, which is, that *some of us have been so brought to recognize the work of Christ that we are saved by it;* because, to confess the truth, there are some of us who were very unlikely subjects (speaking after the manner of men) to be saved. Probably, each saved person here did think himself the most unlikely one ever to be saved; I know that I thought so concerning myself. You remember the story of a Scotchman who went to see Mr. Rowland Hill, and who sat and looked him in the face for a long while, till the good old minister asked him, "What are you looking at?" He replied, "I have been studying the lines of your face." "What do you make of them?" asked Rowland; and the answer was, "I was thinking what a great vagabond you would have been if the grace of God had not met with you." "That thought has often struck me," said Rowland; and a similar thought has often struck some of us. If we had not been converted, wouldn't we have led others into sin? Wouldn't we have invented fresh pleasures of vice and folly? Who would have stopped us? We had daring enough for anything, enough even to have bearded the very devil himself if we had thought that some new vice could have been invented, or some fresh pleasure of sin could have been discovered. But now that God has made us yield, "by sovereign grace subdued," and brought us to his feet, and put on us the chains which now we gladly welcome, and which we long to wear for ever, O come, and let us sing unto the Lord a new song, for he hath done marvellous things for us; "his right hand, and his holy arm, hath gotten him the victory!" Dear child of God, if there be special grace in your case, as I know you feel that there has been, there ought to be special honour given to Christ by you. Everyone who is saved ought to live a very special life,—an extraordinary life.

If you were an extraordinary sinner, or have been, in some way or other, an extraordinary debtor to divine love, may there be some extraordinary devotion, extraordinary consecration, extraordinary faith, extraordinary liberality, extraordinary loving kindness, or something else about you in which the traces of that marvellous right hand of God and his holy arm will be plainly manifested!

The last thing I will speak about is this, *there is something marvellous in the joy which we, who have believed in the victory wrought by Christ, have received.* Probably all of you have sung that song of which the refrain is,—

"I am so glad that Jesus loves me."

That refrain is very monotonous, yet I think I should like to sing it all night, and should not wish to leave off even when the morning broke.

"I am so glad that Jesus loves me."

You may turn it over, and over, and over, and over, as long as ever you like, but you will never find anything that makes you so glad as that thought, "Jesus loves me;" and you will never find that the sweetness of that thought, "Jesus loves me," will ever be exhausted. Sinner, if you only knew the blessedness of the life of Christ, you would be glad enough to run away from your own life, and run to share ours in him! We have peace like a river, we can leave all our cares and our burdens with our God. We are just where we love most to be,—in the bosom of our Heavenly Father, and the Spirit of adoption makes us feel perfectly at home with him. We can say, "Return unto thy rest, O my soul, for the Lord hath dealt bountifully with thee!" We are in perfect safety, for who is he that can destroy those whom Christ protects? We have got into peace even with our own conscience. We have also a blessed prospect for the future; we shall be borne along upon the wings of divine providence until we exchange them for the wings of angels. We have a heaven below, and we are looking for a still better heaven above.

"All that remains for me
Is but to love and sing,
And wait until the angels come
To bear me to the King."

This is the lower part of the choir; some of the singers are up in the galleries, and we are learning here the notes that we shall sing above. Come, beloved, let us make these sinners long to share our joys. If any of you saints have been moaning and groaning of late, get into your proper condition. Begin to tune up, and praise the Lord with all your might till the ungodly shall say, "After all, there is something sweeter and brighter and better in the lives of these Christians than we have ever known in ours. But whether you will rejoice or not, my soul doth magnify the Lord, and my spirit doth rejoice in God my Saviour; and so I will, by his help, till death suspends these mortal songs, or melts them into the songs immortal before the throne. God bless you, brethren and sisters, for Christ's sake! Amen.

9. Christ's Joy and Ours

"These things have I spoken unto you, that my joy might remain in you, and that your joy might be full."—John xv. 11.

THERE is a sentence, which has crept in among our common proverbs, so that it is repeated as if it were altogether true,—" Man was made to mourn." There is a truth in that sentence; but there is also a falsehood in it. Man was not originally made to mourn; he was made to rejoice. The garden of Eden was his place of happy abode; and, so long as he continued obedient to God, nothing grew in that garden which could cause him sorrow. For his delight, the flowers breathed out their perfume. For his delight, the landscapes were full of beauty, and the rivers rippled over golden sands. God made human beings, as he made his other creatures, to be happy. They are capable of happiness, they are in their right element when they are happy; and now that Jesus Christ has come to restore the ruins of the Fall, he has come to bring back to us the old joy,—only it shall be even sweeter and deeper than it could have been if we had never lost it. A Christian has never fully realized what Christ came to make him until he has grasped the joy of the Lord. Christ wishes his people to be happy. When they are perfect, as he will make them in due time, they shall also be perfectly happy. As heaven is the place of pure holiness, so is it the place of unalloyed happiness; and in proportion as we get ready for heaven, we shall have some of the joy which belongs to heaven, and it is our Saviour's will that even now his joy should remain in us, and that our joy should be full.

I. My first remark upon the text will be this, ALL THAT JESUS SPEAKS IS MEANT TO PRODUCE JOY IN HIS PEOPLE: "These things have I spoken unto you, that my joy might remain in you."

If you will read through the chapter from which our text is taken, and also the chapter which precedes it, you will see the nature of the words which Jesus Christ speaks to his people. *Sometimes they*

are words of instruction. He talks to us that we may know the
truth, and the meaning of the truth; but his object is that, knowing
the truth, we may have joy in it. I will not say that the more a
Christian knows, the more joy he has; but I can truly say that
ignorance often hides from us many wells of delight of which we
might otherwise drink, and that, all other things being equal, the
best-instructed Christian will be the happiest man. He will know
the truth, and the truth will make him free. The truth will kill
a thousand fears which ignorance would have fostered within him.
The knowledge of the love of God, the knowledge of the full atonement made on Calvary, the knowledge of the eternal covenant, the
knowledge of the immutable faithfulness of Jehovah,—indeed, all
knowledge which reveals God in his relationship to his people,—will
tend to create comfort in the hearts of the saints. Be not, therefore, careless about Scriptural doctrine; study the Word, and seek
to understand the mind of the Spirit as revealed in it, for this
blessed Book was written for your learning, that "through patience
and comfort of the Scriptures you might have hope." If you are
diligent students of the Word, you will find that you have good
reason to rejoice in the Lord under all circumstances.

But sometimes our Lord also spoke *words of warning*. In this
chapter, we find him telling his disciples that they were branches of
a vine, and that branches which bore no fruit had to be cut off, and
cast into the fire. At first sight, it seems to us that there is
nothing consoling in such words as those, they sound sharply in our
ears, and make us start, and be afraid, and ask ourselves, "Are we
bearing fruit?" Well, brethren and sisters, but such heart-
searching as that is eminently beneficial, and tends to deepen in us
true joy. Christ would not have us rejoice with the false joy of
presumption, so he takes the sharp knife, and cuts that joy away.
Joy on a false basis would prevent us from having true joy; and,
therefore, the Master gives us the sharp and cutting word that we
may be sound in the faith, that we may be sound in the life of God,
and that so the joy we may get may be worth having,—not the
mere surf and foam of a wave that is driven with the wind and
tossed, but the solid foundation of the Rock of Ages.

Our Lord also tells us that even the branches that bear fruit will
have to be pruned that they may bring forth more fruit.
"Unpleasant truth that!" somebody might say; "it will give me
no joy to know that I shall have to endure the knife of correction
and affliction." Yes, dear brother, but "tribulation worketh
patience; and patience, experience; and experience, hope: and
hope maketh not ashamed; because the love of God is shed abroad
in our hearts by the Holy Ghost which is given unto us." So,
beginning rather high up in this pedigree, you get to joy at last,
and get to it by the only right method. To try to sail up to joy
by the balloon of fancy, is dangerous work; but to mount up to it
by Jacob's ladder, every round of which God has placed at the
proper distance, is to climb to heaven by the safe road which he
has appointed. There is nothing which the Lord Jesus says to us,
by way of warning, which does not guard us against sorrow, conduct

us away from danger, and points us to the path of safety. If we will but listen to these words of warning, they will thus guide us to the truest happiness that mortals can ever find either here or hereafter.

You will notice, as you read the chapter, that our Lord, in addition to words of instruction and words of warning, utters *some very humbling words.* I think that is a very humbling verse in which he says, "As the branch cannot bear fruit of itself, except it abide in the vine; no more can ye, except ye abide in me." But it is good for us to be humbled and brought low. The Valley of Humiliation has always struck me as being the most beautiful place in the whole of the pilgrimage which John Bunyan describes. To see that shepherd boy sitting down among the sheep, and to hear him playing upon his pipe, and singing,—

> " He that is down need fear no fall,
> He that is low no pride ;
> He that is humble ever shall
> Have God to be his Guide ;"—

teaches us that, to be brought down to our true condition of nothingness before God, and made to feel our entire dependence upon the power of the Holy Spirit, is the true way to promote in us a joy which angels themselves might envy. Be thankful, therefore, beloved, whenever you read the Scripture, whether it instructs you, or warns you, or humbles you. Say to yourself, " Somehow or other, this tends to my present and eternal joy, and therefore will I give the more earnest heed to it lest by any means I should lose the blessing it is intended to convey to me."

The chapter also abounds in gracious *words of promise,* such as this : " If ye abide in me, and my words abide in you, ye shall ask what ye will, and it shall be done unto you." There are other promises here, every one of which is full of consolation to the children of God. Are any of you lacking in joy at this time ? Do you feel dull and heavy of heart ? Are you depressed and tried ? Then listen to what Jesus Christ says here : " These things have I spoken unto you, that my joy might remain in you, and that your joy might be full." What are the things that he says to you in other parts of his Word ? He says, " Take therefore no thought for the morrow ; for the morrow shall take thought for the things of itself." " Let not your heart be troubled : ye believe in God, believe also in me." " My sheep hear my voice, and I know them, and they follow me : and I give unto them eternal life ; and they shall never perish, neither shall any pluck them out of my hand." In this strain does our Lord graciously talk to us ; do not let him talk to us in vain. My brethren, do not suffer his precious promises to fall upon your ears as the good seed fell upon the rocky or stony soil. The promise of harvest gives joy to the earth. Rob not your Lord of the sheaves which he deserves to gather from your heart and life ; but believe his Word, rest upon it, and rejoice in it, realizing that his words of promise are meant to bring you great joy.

So are *his words of precept.* This chapter contains many of them, for he tells us that it is his command that we should love our brethren, and also that we should continue in his love. He gives us many precepts of that kind, and every precept in God's Word is a signpost pointing out the road to joy. The commandments upon the tables of stone seem very hard, even though cut by the finger of God himself, and the granite on which they are engraved is hard and cold; but the precepts of the Lord Jesus are tender and gracious, and bring us joy and life. As you read them, you may be quite sure of two things; that is, if Christ denies you anything, it is not good for you; and if Christ commands you to do anything, obedience will promote your highest welfare. O child of God, never cavil at any precept of your Lord! If your proud flesh should rebel, pray it down; for, rest assured that, if you were so selfish as only to wish to do that which would promote your own happiness, it would be the path of wisdom to be obedient to your Lord and Master. I repeat what I said just now. The precepts of Christ are signposts indicating the way to joy. If you keep his commandments, you shall abide in his love; and if you carefully watch his eye, as the handmaidens watch the eye of their mistress, so as to do at once all that he bids you do, you shall have the peace of God flowing into your soul like a river, and that peace shall never fail to bring you solid and lasting joy.

II. Now, secondly, I gather from the text that, WHEN OUR LORD JESUS CHRIST JOYS IN US, THEN WE ALSO HAVE JOY.

This meaning of the text is the interpretation given to it by several of the early fathers: "These things have I spoken unto you, that my joy might remain in you." "That is to say," say they, "that I may rejoice over you, and rejoice in you, and be pleased with you, and that so your joy may be full." I am not certain that this is the meaning of the text, nor am I sure that it is not; but, anyhow, it is a very blessed truth. It means this. A child knows that its father loves it; but while it is quite sure that its father will never cease to love it, it also knows that, if it is disobedient, the father will be displeased and grieved. But the obedient child gives pleasure to its father by its obedience; and when it has done so, it receives pleasure itself from that very fact. There used to be servants, in the olden time,—and I suppose there are some now, —who were so attached to their masters that, if they gave satisfaction to them, they were perfectly satisfied; but the least word of displeasure from their master wounded them to the very heart. Perhaps a better illustration may be found in the nearer and dearer relationship of the wife and the husband. The wife, if she has pleased her husband, is delighted in the joy which she has given to him; but if, by any means, she has displeased him, she is unhappy until she has removed the cause of his displeasure, and has again given him joy. Now I know that my Lord Jesus loves me, and that he will never do anything else but love me. Yet he may not be always pleased with me; and when he has no joy in me, my joy also goes if I have a heart that is true towards him; but when he has joy in me, when he can rejoice in me, then is my joy also full; and every one of you, whom the Lord has loved, will find this to be true,—that, in proportion as Jesus Christ can look upon you with joy as obedient and faithful to him, in that proportion will your conscience be at ease, and your mind will find joy in the thought that you are acceptable unto him.

What are the ways in which we can really please Christ Jesus, and so have joy in Christ's pleasure? According to the chapter before us, *we please him when we abide in him:* "If ye abide in me, and my words abide in you, ye shall ask what ye will, and it shall be done unto you." If you sometimes abide in Christ, and sometimes turn away from him, you will give him no pleasure; but if he be the indispensable Companion of your daily life,—if you are unhappy should even a cloud come between you and your Lord,—if you feel that you must be as closely connected with him as the limb is with the head, or as the branch is with the stem, then you will please him, and he will take delight in your fellowship. Fervent love to Christ is very pleasing to him; but the chilly, lukewarm love of Laodicea is nauseous to him, so that he says, "Because thou art lukewarm, and neither cold nor hot, I will spue thee out of my mouth." If you continue, day by day, to walk with God carefully and prayerfully, and to abide in Christ continually, he will look upon you with eyes of satisfaction and delight, and will see in you the reward of his soul-travail; and you, being conscious that you are giving joy to him, will find that your own cup of joy is also full to overflowing. What greater joy can a man have than to feel that he is pleasing Christ? My fellow-creatures may condemn what I do; but if Christ accepts it, it matters nothing to me how many may condemn it. They may misrepresent and misjudge me, and impute wrong motives to me, and sneer and snarl at me; but if I can keep up constant and unbroken communion with the Christ of God, what cause have I for sorrow? Nay, if he be joyful in us, then our joy shall remain in us, and shall be full.

Our Lord Jesus has also told us that *he has joy in us when we bring forth much fruit:* "Herein is my Father glorified, that ye bear much fruit; so shall ye be my disciples;" that is to say, "I will recognize in you the evidence of true discipleship with satisfaction and delight." Brethren and sisters in Christ, are we bringing forth much fruit unto God? Are you called to suffer? Then do you, in your suffering, bring forth the fruit of patience? Or, are you strong and in robust health? Then are you, with that health and strength, rendering to the Lord the fruit of holy activity? Are you doing all you can for the Lord Jesus, who has done so much for you? You have received much from him; are you yielding any adequate return to him? It is little enough when it is what we call much; but, oh, how little it is when it is little in our own estimation! But when our Lord Jesus Christ sees us doing much for God, he is pleased with us, as the gardener is when, having planted a tree, and digged about it, and manured it, and pruned it, he sees it at last covered with golden fruit. He is pleased with his fruitful tree, and Christ is pleased with his fruit-bearing disciples. Are we making Christ glad in this fashion? If so, our own joy shall be full. I am not surprised that some Christians have

so little joy when I remember how little joy they are giving to
Jesus, because they are bringing forth such a little fruit to his
praise and glory. Brethren and sisters, see ye to this matter, I
pray you. If I cannot enforce this truth with the power that it
deserves, may the Holy Spirit cause the truth to come home with
power to your hearts!

Our Lord also tells us that *he has joy in us when we keep his
commandments:* "If ye keep my commandments, ye shall abide in
my love; even as I have kept my Father's commandments, and abide
in his love. These things have I spoken unto you, that my joy
might remain in you, and that your joy might be full. This is my
commandment, That ye love one another, as I have loved you." He
that walks carefully in the matter of obedience to Christ's commands,
wishing never to do anything offensive to him, asking for a tender
conscience that he may be at once aware when he is doing wrong,
and earnestly desiring to leave no duty undone,—such a man as
that must be happy. He may not laugh much; he may have very
little to say when in frivolous company; but there is a joy that
laughter would but mock, there is a sacred mirth within to which
the merriment of fools is but as the crackling of thorns under a
pot; and the man with a tender conscience has that joy, the careful
walker has that joy, the man who, when he puts his head upon his
pillow at night, can feel, "I have not been all that I want to be;
but, still, I have aimed at holiness, I have tried to curb my passions,
I have sought to find out my Master's will, and in every point to do
it." Such a man sleeps sweetly; and if he wakes, there is music in
his heart; and such a man, whatever the trials of life may be, has
abundant sources of joy within himself. He is pleasing to Christ;
Christ joys in him, and his joy is full.

And *this is peculiarly the case with those who love the brethren.*
There are some who do not love their brethren at all; or if they do,
they love themselves a great deal more. They are very apt to
judge and to condemn their brethren. If they can find a little
fault, they magnify it; and if they can find none, they invent some.
I know some persons, who seem to be, by nature, qualified to be
monks or hermits, living quite alone; according to their notion of
things, they are much too good for society. No church is pure
enough for them; no ministry can profit them; no one else can
reach as high as the wonderful position to which, in their self-
conceit, they fancy that they have attained. Let none of us
be of that sort. Many of the children of God are far better than we
are, and the worst one in his family has some points in which he is
better than we are. I feel, sometimes, as though I would give my
eyes to be as sure of heaven as the most obscure and the least in
all the family of God; and I think that such times may come to
some of you if you imagine yourselves to be so great and good. You
strong cattle, that push with horn and with shoulder, and that drive
back the weak ones, the Lord may say to you, "Get you gone; you
belong not to me, for my people are not thus rough and boastful,—
not thus proud and haughty; but I look to the man who is humble,
to him who has a contrite spirit, and who trembles at my Word."

Did you every try to pray to God under the influence of a consciousness of possessing the higher life? Did you ever try to pray to God that way? If you ever did, I do not think you will do it a second time. I tried it once, but I am not likely to repeat the experiment. I thought I would try to pray to God in that fashion, but it did not seem to come naturally from me; and when I had done so, I thought I heard somebody at a distance saying, "God be merciful to me a sinner," and he went home to his house justified; and then I had to tear off my Pharisaic robes, and get back to where the poor publican had been standing, for his place and his prayer suited me admirably. I cannot make out what has happened to some of my brethren, who fancy themselves so wonderfully good. I wish the Lord would strip them of their self-righteousness, and let them see themselves as they really are in his sight. Their fine notions concerning the higher life would soon vanish then. Brethren, the highest life I ever hope to reach to, this side of heaven, is to say from my very soul,—

> "I the chief of sinners am,
> But Jesus died for me."

I have not the slightest desire to suppose that I have advanced in the spiritual life many stages beyond my brethren. As long as I trust simply to the blood and righteousness of Christ, and think nothing of myself, I believe that I shall continue to be pleasing to the Lord Jesus Christ, that his joy will be in me, and that my joy will be full.

III. Now, thirdly, I think we may gather from the text that THE JOY WHICH JESUS GIVES TO HIS PEOPLE IS HIS OWN JOY: "That *my* joy might remain in you."

I daresay you have noticed that a man cannot communicate to another any joy except that of which he is himself conscious. Here is a man who is rich; he can tell you the joy of riches, but he cannot give that joy to a poor man. Here is another man who takes delight in all sorts of foolery; he can tell you the joy of nonsense, but he cannot go beyond that. So, when Jesus gives us joy, he gives us his own joy; and what, think you, is that? I must put it very briefly.

The joy of Jesus is, first, *the joy of abiding in his Father's love.* He knows that his Father loves him,—that he never did anything else but love him,—that he loved him or ever the earth was,—that he loved him when he was in the manger, and that he loved him when he was on the cross. Now that is the joy which Christ gives to you, the joy of knowing that your Father loves you. Let me stop a little while, that you, who really are believers in the Lord Jesus Christ, may just roll that sweet morsel under your tongue,—the everlasting God loves you! I have known the time when I have felt as if I could leap up at the very thought of God's love to me. That he pities you, and cares for you, you can understand; but that he loves you,—well, if that does not make your joy full, there is nothing that can. It ought to fill us with delight to know that we are loved of the Lord, with an everlasting and infinite love, even as

Jesus Christ is loved. "The Father himself loveth you," declares Christ; so, surely, you share Christ's joy, and that fact should make your own joy full.

Christ's joy was also *the joy of hallowed friendship.* He said to his disciples, "Henceforth I call you not servants; for the servant knoweth not what his Lord doeth: but I have called you friends; for all things that I have heard of my Father I have made known unto you." The friends of Jesus are those who are taken by him into most intimate fellowship,—to lean upon his breast, and to become his constant companions. Our Lord Jesus Christ has great joy in being on the most friendly terms with his people, and have not you also great joy in being on such friendly terms with him? What higher joy do you want or can you have? I have heard a man say, very boastfully, that he once dined with Lord So-and-so; and another, just for the sake of showing off, spoke of his friend, Sir John somebody or other. But you have the Lord Jesus Christ as your personal Friend, your Divine Companion; you are going to sit and feast with him presently at his own table. He calls you no more his servant, but his friend; does not that fact make you rejoice with exceeding joy? What is your heart made of if it does not leap with joy at such an assurance as that? You are beloved of the Lord, and a friend of the Son of God! Kings might well be willing to give up their crowns if they could have such bliss as this.

Moreover, *our Lord Jesus felt an intense delight in glorifying his Father.* It was his constant joy to bring glory to his Father. Have you ever felt the joy of glorifying God, or do you now feel joy in Christ because he has glorified his Father? I solemnly declare that, if Christ would not save me, I must love him for what he has done to exhibit the character of God. I have sometimes thought that, if he were to drive me out of doors, I would stand there in the cold, and say, "Do what thou wilt with me; crush me if thou wilt; but I will always love thee, for there never was another such as thou art, never one who so well deserved my love, and so fully won my affection and admiration as thou hast done." How gloriously has Christ rolled away the great load of human sin, adequately recompensed the claims of divine justice, and magnified the law, and made it honourable! He took the greatest possible delight in doing this; it was for the joy that was set before him that he endured the cross, despising the shame. Let that joy be yours also; rejoice that the law is honoured, that justice is satisfied, and that free grace is gloriously displayed in the atoning work of the Lord Jesus Christ. It was the joy of Christ that he should finish the work which his Father gave him to do; and he has finished it, and therefore he is glad; will not you also rejoice in his finished work? You have not to put a single stitch to the robe of righteousness which he has wrought; it is woven from the top throughout, and absolutely perfect in every respect. You have not to contribute even a quarter of a penny to the ransom price for your redemption, for it is paid to the uttermost farthing. The great redemptive work is for ever finished, and Christ has done it all. He is Alpha, and he is Omega; he is the Author and he is also the Finisher of our

faith. Sit down, my brethren and sisters in Christ, and just feed
on this precious truth. Surely, this is the "feast of fat things, a
feast of wines on the lees, of fat things full of marrow, of wines on
the lees well refined," of which the prophet Isaiah long ago wrote.
I see thee, Lord Jesus, with thy foot upon the dragon's neck; I see
thee with death and hell beneath thy feet; I see the glory that
adorns thy triumphant brow as thou waitest till the whole earth
shall acknowledge thee as King; for thou hast once for all said,
"It is finished," and finished it certainly is; and shall not my poor
heart rejoice because thou hast finished it, and finished it for me?

IV. My last observation is that, WHEN CHRIST COMMUNICATES HIS
JOY TO HIS PEOPLE, IT IS A JOY WHICH REMAINS, AND A JOY WHICH
IS FULL.

No other joy remains. There is a great deal of very proper joy
in many families when children are born, yet how many little
coffins are followed by weeping mothers! There is joy when God
fills the barn, and very properly so, for a bountiful harvest should
make men glad; but the winter soon comes, with its cold, and
dark, and dreary weather. But, brethren, *when we get the joy of
the Lord, it remains.* Why? Because the cause of it remains. The
rill will continue as long as the spring runs; and the joy of a
Christian is one that never can alter, because the cause of it never
alters. God's love never changes towards his people; the atonement never loses its efficacy; our Lord Jesus Christ never ceases his
intercession; his acceptableness with God on our behalf never varies;
the promises do not change; the covenant is not like the moon,—
sometimes waxing and sometimes waning. Oh, no; if you rejoice
with Christ's joy to-day, you will have the same cause for rejoicing
to-morrow, and for ever, and for evermore, for he says that his joy
shall remain in you.

Then, next, *this joy is full joy.* Then, dear brethren, if our joy
is full, two things are very clear; first, there is no room for any
more joy; and, secondly, there is no room for any sorrow. When
a man gets to know the love of God to him, he is so full of delight
that he does not want any more joy. The pleasures of this world
lose all their former charm. When a man has eaten all he can eat,
you may set whatever you like before him, but he has no appetite
for it. "Enough is as good as a feast," we say. When a man is
forgiven by God, and knows that he is saved, the joy of the Lord
enters his soul, and he says, "You may take all other joys, and
do what you like with them. I have my God, my Saviour, and I
want no more." Then, ambition ceases, lust is quiet, covetousness
is dead, and desires, that once roamed abroad, now stay at home.
The saved one says, "My God, thou art enough for me; what more
can I require? Since thou hast said to me, 'I love thee,' and my
heart has responded, 'My God, I love thee, too,' I have more true
wealth at my disposal than if I had all the mines of the Indies under
my control."

There is, also, no longer any room for sorrow, for if Christ's
joy has filled us, where can sorrow come? "But the man has lost
his gold." "Yes," he says, "but if the Lord likes to take it from

me, let him have it." " But the man is bereaved of those that are
very dear to him, as Job was." Yet he says, " The Lord gave, and
the Lord hath taken away; blessed be the name of the Lord." When
a man consciously realizes the love of God in his soul, he cannot
want more than that. I wish that all of us had that realization;
for, then, our joy would be so great that we should have no room
left for sorrow.

Now, dear brethren and sisters, as you come to the table of your
Lord in this spirit, you will feel so full of joy that you will be too
full for words. People really full of joy do not usually talk much.
A person, who is carrying a glass that is full to the brim, does not
go dancing along like one who has nothing to carry. He is
very quiet and steady, for he does not want to spill the contents
of the glass. So, the man who has the joy of the Lord filling his soul
is often quiet; he cannot say much about it. I have even known
that joy to get so full that we have scarcely known whether we have
been in the body or out of the body. Pain, sickness, depression of
spirit,—all seem to have been taken right away; and the man has
had so clear a view of Christ, and his mind has been so abstracted
from everything else, that, afterwards, it has almost seemed like a
dream to him to have felt the love of God in its almighty power,
lifting him above all surrounding circumstances.

Then, dear brethren, if it be so with us, the joy of the Lord will
be much too full for us ever to forget it. If, at this very moment,
our soul is filled with Christ's joy, it is possible that, twenty or
thirty years hence, any one of us may be able to say, " I remember
that first Sabbath night in the year 1875 at the Tabernacle; my
Lord then met with me, looked into my soul, and saw there was
a void there, and he poured his own heart's joy into me until my
soul could not hold any more." And, perhaps, in some dark
time in the future, your present experience will be a great stay
to your soul, and you will recall David's words in a similar case,
" O my God, my soul is cast down within me: therefore will I
remember thee from the land of Jordan, and of the Hermonites,
from the hill Mizar;" and you will say, " Though, now, deep calleth
unto deep at the noise of thy waterspouts, the remembrance of that
bright season causes me to know that thou dost not forsake those on
whom thy love has once been set." Come close to your Lord,
beloved. I delight to come very near to him. To touch the hem
of his garment, is enough for sinners; but it is not enough for saints.
We want to sit at his feet with Mary, and to lay our heads upon
his bosom as John did. O ye unconverted ones, look to Jesus; for,
if ye look to him, ye shall live! But as for you who are converted,
a look will not be enough for you. You want to keep on gazing at
him, and for him to keep on gazing at you, till he shall say to you,
" Thou hast ravished my heart, my sister, my spouse; thou hast
ravished my heart with one of thine eyes, with one chain of thy
neck;" and you also shall say, " He brought me to the banqueting
house, and his banner over me was love. Stay me with flagons,
comfort me with apples: for I am sick of love." Oh, that there
might now be such sweet fellowship between Christ and all his

blood-besprinkled ones that, if we cannot pass the portals of heaven, we shall be very near them; and if we cannot hear the songs of the angels, at any rate they will hear ours; and if we cannot look within, and behold their joys, let us at least tempt them to look without, and see ours, and half wish that they might be allowed to sit with us at this communion table, though that is an honour reserved for sinners saved by sovereign grace, for—

> " Never did angels taste above
> Redeeming grace and dying love."

Thus may the Master smile on you, my dearly-beloved, and make you to be such eminent saints that he can have great joy in you; for, then, his joy shall remain in you, and your joy shall be full.

How I wish that everybody here knew my dear Lord and Master! I tell you, who do not know Christ, and do not experimentally know what true religion is, that five minutes' realization of the love of Christ would be better for you than a million years of your present choicest delights. There is more brightness in the dark side of Christ than in the brightest side of this poor world. I would sooner lie on a bed, and ache in every limb, with the death-sweat standing on my brow, by the month and year together, persecuted, despised, and forsaken, poor and naked, with the dogs to lick my sores, and the devils to tempt my soul, and have Christ for my Friend, than I would sit in the palaces of wicked kings, with all their wealth, and luxury, and pampering, and sin. Even at our worst estate, it is better to be God's dog than the devil's darling; it is better to have the crumbs and the mouldy crusts that fall from Christ's table for the dogs than to sit at the head of princely banquets with the ungodly. "I had rather be a doorkeeper in the house of my God, than to dwell in the tents of wickedness." God bless you, and save you; and he will do so if you trust in Jesus his dear Son. As soon as you trust in Jesus, you are saved. God grant that you may do so this very hour, for his dear name's sake! Amen.

10. The Singing Army

"And Judah gathered themselves together to ask help of the Lord."—2 Chronicles, xx. 4.

JERUSALEM was startled by sudden news. There had for a great while been quiet preparations made in the distant countries beyond Jordan. Upon its mountains Edom had been getting ready : the workshops of Petra had been ringing with the hammer; the enemies of Israel had been beating their pruning hooks into spears and swords, and they were now coming down in hordes. There were three great nations, and these were assisted by the odds and ends of all the nations round about, so that a great company eager for plunder was drawn up in battle. They had heard about the riches of the temple at Jerusalem; they knew that the people of Judea had for years been flourishing, and they were now coming to kill and to destroy and to sack and to plunder. They were like the grasshoppers or the locusts for multitude. What were the people of God to do? How were these poor Judeans to defend themselves? Their immediate resort was to their God. They do not appear to have looked up their armour and their swords with any particular anxiety. The fact was the case was so altogether hopeless as far as they were concerned, that it was no use looking to anything beneath the skies, and as they were driven from all manifest earthly resorts they were compelled to lift up their eyes to God; and their godly king Jehoshaphat aided them in so doing. A general fast was proclaimed, and the preparation to meet the hosts of Moab, Ammon and Edom was prayer. No doubt if the Ammonites had heard of it they would have laughed, Edom would have scoffed at it, and Moab would have cursed those that made supplication. "What! do they suppose that their prayers can defeat us?" would have been the sneer of their adversaries. Yet this was Israel's artillery: this was their eighty-one ton gun: when it was ready it would throw one bolt, and only one, and that would crush three nations at once. God's people resorted only to the arm invisible—the arm omnipotent—and they did well and wisely.

Now, if the Lord shall teach us to imitate them, and by his grace enable us in doing it, we shall have learnt a great lesson. The preacher needs to learn it as much as anybody, and he prays that each one of you may be also scholars in the school of faith, and become very proficient in the divine art of prayer and praise.

I.   First, then, HOW THEY ASKED HELP? They asked their help, as you know, by a general fast and prayer, but I mean, what was the style of that prayer in which they approached the Lord?

And the reply is, first, *they asked help, expressing their confidence.* "O Lord God of our fathers, art not thou God in heaven? and rulest not thou over all the kingdoms of the heathen? and in thine hand is there not power and might, so that none is able to withstand thee?" If we begin by doubting, our prayer will limp. Faith is the tendon of Achilles, and if that be cut it is not possible for us to wrestle with God, but as long as we have that strong sinew, that mighty tendon unhurt, we can prevail with God in prayer. It is a rule of the kingdom, though God often goes beyond it, "According to thy faith be it done unto thee." I have known him give us a hundred times as much as our faith, but, brethren, I have never known him give us less. That could not possibly be. This is his minimum rule, I may say, "According to thy faith be it unto thee." When, therefore, in time of trouble you ask help of God, ask it believing that he is able to give it; ask it expecting that he will bestow it. Do not grieve the Spirit of God by unworthy doubts and mistrusts; these things will be like fiery arrows in your own soul and drink up the very life of your strength. However hard the struggle and difficult the trial, if thou seekest the Lord, seek him in the confidence he deserves.

Then *they sought God, pleading his past acts.* This is a fashion of prayer which has been very common among the saints, and it has proved to be very potent. "Art not thou our God, who didst drive out the inhabitants of this land before thy people Israel, and gavest it to the seed of Abraham thy friend for ever?" Remember what God has done for you, and then say, as a sweet refrain, "Jesus Christ, the same yesterday, to-day, and for ever." When you are praying, recollect what he was yesterday if you cannot see that he is comfortable towards you to-day. If there be no present manifestations of divine favour, recall the former days—the days of old —the years of the right hand of the Most High. He has been gracious unto you; can you tell how gracious? He has abounded towards you in lovingkindness, and tenderness, and faithfulness; he has never been a wilderness or a land of drought unto you. Well, then, if in six troubles he has delivered thee, wilt thou not trust him for seven? If you get to sixty troubles, cannot you trust him for sixty-one? You have been carried, some of you, I see, till grey hairs are on your head. How long do you expect to live? Do you think you have got an odd ten years left? Well, do you think that the Lord who has blest you seventy years will not keep you the other ten. We say that we ought always to trust a man until he deceives us. We reckon a man honest, till we find him otherwise. Let it be so with God, I beseech you. Since we have found him good, faithful, true, kind, tender, let us not think hardly of him now that we have come into straits, but let us come to him thus, and say, " Art not thou our God? Didst not thou bring us up out of the horrible pit and out of the miry clay? Didst thou not bring us up out of the Egypt of our sin? Surely thou hast not brought us into the wilderness to destroy us? Wilt thou leave us now? True, we are unworthy, but so we always were, and if thou didst want a reason for leaving us thou hast had ten thousand reasons long ago. Lord, do not be wroth very sore with thy servants, and cast us not away." That is the style of pleading which prevails. Imitate these men of old, who asked help by recalling the past.

Proceeding a little farther in their prayer, we see that *they pleaded the promise of God*, which promise was made at the time when Solomon dedicated the temple. " That if, when evil cometh upon us, we cry unto thee in our affliction, then thou wilt hear and help." He that getteth the promise of God and graspeth God with the promise—he does, and must prevail. I have known sometimes a man unable to grasp anything; the object has slipped away, his hand has been slippery too, and I have seen him as he has taken up some sand in his hand, and then he has been able to get a grip. I like to plunge my hand into the promises, and then I find myself able to grasp with a grip of determination the mighty faithfulness of God. An omnipotent plea with God is : " Do as thou hast said." You know how a man nails you when he brings your very words before you. "There," says he, "that is what you said you would do. Of your own free will you pledged yourself to do this." Why then you cannot get away from it, for it is the way with the saints that if they swear to their own hurt they change not; they must be true to the words they speak even if it be to their own damage. Of the saints' Master it is always true. "Hath he said and shall he not do it? or hath he spoken and shall he not make it good? " Here then is a mighty instrument to be used in prayer, " Lord, thou hast said this or that, thou hast said it, now do as thou hast said. Thou hast said, 'Many are the afflictions of the righteous, but the Lord delivereth him out of them all.' Thou hast said, 'He shall deliver thee in six troubles, and in seven there shall no evil touch thee.' Thou hast said, 'Surely in blessing I will bless thee.' Thou hast said, ' The Lord thy God is with thee whithersoever thou goest.' Thou hast said, ' Thy shoes shall be iron and brass, and as thy days so shall thy strength be.' Lord, there is thy promise for it." With such a plea you must prevail with a faithful God.

Again, as these people asked for help *they confessed their own unhappy condition*. There is a great power in that. One of the strongest pleas with generosity is the urgency of poverty, and one of the most prevailing arguments to be used in prayer with God is a truthful statement of our condition—a confession of our sad estate. So they said to the Lord these words, "O our God, wilt thou not judge them? for we have no might against this great company that cometh against us; neither know we what to do: but our eyes are upon thee." They had no might, and they had no plan. "We have no might, neither know we what to do." Sometimes even if you cannot do the thing, it is a little comfort to know how it might be done if you had the power, but these perplexed people neither could do it, nor knew how to do it. They were nonplussed. A little nation like Judah, surrounded by these powerful enemies, truly had no might. Their weakness and ignorance were great pleas: the logic was divine. "Neither know we what to do: therefore our eyes are unto thee." It was as if they had said, "If we could do it ourselves, well, thou mightest very well say, 'Go and do it. What did I give you the strength for, but that you could use the strength in doing it?' But when we have got no strength, neither know we what to do, we come and just lay the case down at thy feet and say, 'There it is; our eyes are upon thee.'" Perhaps you think that is not praying. I tell you it is the most powerful form of prayer, just to set your case before God, just to lay bare all your sorrow and all your needs, and then say, "Lord, there it is." You know a man must not beg in the streets of London; the police will not have it, and I daresay that is a very wise regulation. But what does the needy man do? Have not you seen him? He is dressed like a countryman, and looks half-starved, and his knees can be seen through an old pair of corduroys as he stoops. He does not beg, not he: he only sits down at the corner of the road. He knows quite well that the very sight of his condition is enough. There are one or two persons about the streets of London whose faces are a fortune to them; pale, and thin, and woebegone, they appeal more eloquently than words. I was going to say that there is a man who comes to the Tabernacle, who is just of the same sort. I could point him out, but I do not see him now; but he does come here, and the very way in which he shivers, the remarkable manner in which he looks ill, though he is not ill, takes in people who are continually being duped by his appearance. All the world knows that it is the look of the thing, the very appearance and show of sorrow, that prevails with people more than any words that are used. Now, when you cannot pray in words, go and lay bare your sorrow before God: just go and show your soul. Tell God what it is that burdens and distresses you, and you will prevail with the bounteous heart of our God, who is not moved by eloquence of words, and oratory of tongue, but is swift to answer the true oratory, the true eloquence, of real distress, and who is as wise to detect sham misery as to succour real sorrow.

I wonder whether I recall to some of you any particular times of trial. To myself I do. If I do not to you, at any rate, there is one common affliction which has overwhelmed us all, that is the great affliction of sin. When sin, with its multitudinous host of offences, becomes manifest to us under conviction, and we do not know how to meet one single sin or to answer one of a thousand of the charges that might be brought against us; when we feel that we have no might whatever, and perhaps we realise that through sin we have brought ourselves into such peculiar circumstances that we do not know how to get out of it, though we feel that we must get out somehow : when we go to the right that seems blocked up, and the left seems equally closed to us : to go back we dare not : to go forward we cannot—then how wonderfully God clears the way ! In what a marvellous manner we find our enemies all dead that we thought were going to kill us ! and as for those that were going to rob us, we are enriched by them. Instead of taking us for a spoil, there they fall and their spoil becomes our right and we take it home with us rejoicing. Oh, what wonders God can do ! He loves us to state the difficulty we are in, on purpose that when he gets us out of it we may remember that we were in such a condition. It was a real disaster and a time of real trial, and yet the Lord redeemed us from it.

What did they do after asking help, after pleading the promise and confessing their condition? Why, *they expressed their confidence in God*. They said, " Our eyes are upon thee." What did they mean by that? They meant, " Lord, if help does come, it must come from thee. We are looking to thee for it. It cannot come from anywhere else, so we look to thee. But we believe it will come, men will not look for that which they know will not come. We feel sure it will come, but we do not know how, so we are looking; we do not know when, but we are looking. We do not know what thou wouldest have us to do, but as the servant looks to her mistress, so are we looking to thee, Lord. Lord, we are looking." It is a grand posture that. Do you not know that is the way you are saved—by looking unto Jesus? And that is the way you have got to be saved, all the way between here and heaven. Whatever trouble comes, looking is to save you. Looking, often waiting, looking like the weary watcher from the tower when he wants to see the grey tints of the coming morning, when the night is long and he is weary, but still looking. " Our eyes are upon thee." They are full of tears, but still they are upon thee ; they are getting hazy, too, with sleep, but still they are upon thee—such eyes as we have got. We do look to thee. I have sometimes blessed the Lord that he has not said, " See Jesus—see me and be saved." What he has said is, " Look." Sometimes if you cannot see you have done your part if you have looked—looked into the darkness. Lord, that cross of thine, it would give me such joy if I could see it, I cannot quite see it, it looms very indistinctly on my gaze, but I do look. It is looking, you know, that saves, for as we look the eyes get stronger, and we are enlightened. And so in this case they looked, and they found deliverance. God help us, brothers and sisters, to do the same.

That is how they asked help.

II. Now, secondly, HOW THEY RECEIVED HELP.

Their help came to them, first, by a message from God. *They received a fresh assurance of God's goodness.* A new prophet was raised up, and he spoke with new words. " Be not afraid, nor dismayed," he said, " by reason of this great multitude ; for the battle is not yours but God's." Now, in our case, we shall not have a new promise, that would not be possible.

> "What more can he say than to you he hath said,
> You who unto Jesus for refuge have fled."

But you will have that promise sweetly laid home to your soul, and the Spirit of God will bear witness with that promise, and so strengthen and comfort you, that you will get deliverance even before deliverance comes, because it often happens that to be saved from the fear of the trouble is the main business. To be quieted, and calmed, and assured, is really to be saved from the sting of trial; the trial itself is nothing if it does not bring a sting to your soul. If your heart is not troubled, then there is not much trouble in anything else. All the poverty and all the pain in the world would prevail nothing if the evil of it did not enter into the soul and vex it. So, in this emergency, God began to answer his people by quieting them. "Be not afraid nor dismayed, for the battle is not yours but God's: the Lord will be with you."

, As that gracious promise calmed their fears so that they were able without fear to face the impending attack, then *they received distinct direction what to do on the morrow*, which was to be the day of the assault: that direction was, "Go out to meet the foe." How often has God given his people deliverance by quieting them as to their course of action. Already the step they have taken has delivered them before they know it. The Israelites, by then marching out to meet the foe, and marching out with songs and hosannas, as we shall see, were doing the best possible thing to rout their foes. As we have already said, there is no doubt that their enemies were unable to comprehend such a defence as this: they must have supposed that there was some treachery or ambush intended, and so they began to slay each other, and Israel had nothing to do but to keep on singing.

Then came the real providence: *they received actual deliverance.* When the people of Judah came to their foes they found there were no foes. There they lay all stark and dead; none of the men of might could raise their hands against those whom God had favoured. After this fashion will God deliver you, brethren; in answer to prayer he will be your defence. Therefore, sing unto his name. Did not he deliver you thus when you went out to meet the great army of your sins? You saw that Christ had put them away, and your heart danced within you as you said, "There is therefore now no condemnation to them that are in Christ Jesus, for he has slain our sins and they can curse us no more." So has it been with a great many troubles that have appeared to you to be overwhelming: when you have come to them, lo, they have disappeared. They have been cleared out of your way as you have advanced, and you have had nothing to do but to sing and praise the name of the Lord.

III. And now, thirdly, and this is the main point, let us note HOW THEY ACTED AFTER THEY HAD PRAYED AND HEARD GOD'S VOICE. They asked for help, and they had it: how did they then behave?

Well, first, as soon as ever they had an assurance that God would deliver them, *they worshipped.* That is one of the intentions of trial—to revive in us the spirit of devotion and communion with God. And mercy, when it comes on the back of a great trouble, leads us sweetly to prayer. I warrant you there had not been such a piece of worship in all Jerusalem as there was that day, when, after that young son of the Levites had stood and delivered the word of the Lord, the king bowed his head and all the people bowed their heads and did homage to the God of Israel. You could have heard the sound even of the wind among the trees at the time, for they were as hushed and as quiet as you were just now. Oh, when you know the Lord means to deliver you, bow your head and just give him the quiet, deep, solemn worship of your spirit. I do not suppose we shall ever fall into Quakers' worship in our public assemblies, though an occasional experience of it would do you a world of good: to sit still before the Lord, and to adore, and to adore, and to adore again and again, and still again, braces the spirit and clears the soul for the understanding of eternal realities. They worshipped, but why did they do it? They were not delivered. No, but they were sure they were going to be delivered. Their enemies were not dead. No, they were all alive, but they were sure they would be dead, so they had worship, and their devotion rose from trustful and grateful hearts. May we get into a worshipping frame of mind, and be kept in it. Then God will appear for our help.

As soon as ever the worship had closed, or rather ere it had quite closed, *they began to praise.* As we read just now, up went the loud voices of the trained singers under the leadership of the chief musician, and they praised the name of the Lord. They sang, as we do,—

> " For his mercies shall endure,
> Ever faithful, ever sure."

That is the way you should deal with God. Before the deliverance comes, praise him. Praise him for what is coming; adore him for what he is going to do. No song is so sweet, methinks, in the ear of God as the song of a man who blesses him for " grace he has not tasted yet "—for what he has not got, but what he is sure will come. The praise of gratitude for the past is sweet, but that praise is sweeter which adores God for the future in full confidence that it shall be well. Therefore, take down your harps from the willows, O ye people, and praise ye the name of the Lord, though still the fig tree does not blossom and still the cattle die in the stall, and still the sheep perish from the folds ; though there should be to you no income to meet your want, and you should be brought almost to necessity's door, still bless the Lord whose mighty providence cannot fail, and shall not fail, so long as there is one of his children to be provided for. Your song while you are still in distress will be sweet music to the ear of God.

After they had worshipped and sung, the next thing these people did was, to act : *they went forth marching.* If there were unbelievers in Jerusalem, I know what they said. They stood at the gates and they said, "Well, this is foolishness. These Moabites and Ammonites are come to kill you, and they will do it, but you might as well wait till they get at you. You are just going to deliver yourselves up." That would be the idea of unbelief, and that is also what it sometimes seems to our little faith when we go and commit ourselves to God. "What! are you going on your knees to confess your guilt before God and own that you deserve to be lost? Are you going to withdraw every excuse and apology, every trust of your own, and give yourself up, as it were, to destruction?" Yes, that is exactly what to do, and it is the highest wisdom to do it; we are going out of the city marching away according to orders, and if, as you say, we are to give ourselves up, so we will. Perhaps, in your case, you are going to do an action of which everybody else says, "Well, now, that will be very foolish. You should be crafty. You should show a little cunning." "No," say you, "I cannot do other than I am bidden, I must do the right." Probably that will turn out to be the very best thing in the world to have done. The nearest way between any two points is by a straight line, the straight way will always be better than the crooked way. In the long run it is always so. Go right out, then, in the name of God: meet your difficulties calmly and fairly. Do not have any plans or tricks, but just commit yourselves unto God; that is the way by which you may in confidence expect to find deliverance. These people of old went out of the city.

But now, notice again, that as they went out, *they went out singing*. They sang before they left the city, and sang as they left the city, and when the adversary came in sight they began to sing again. The trumpet sounded and the harps rang out their notes, and the minstrels again shouted for joy, and this was the song,—

> "For his mercies shall endure,
> Ever faithful, ever sure."

It must have had a grand significance when they sang that passage, "To him which smote great kings: for his mercy endureth for ever: and slew famous kings: for his mercy endureth for ever: Sihon king of Amorites: for his mercy endureth for ever: and Og the king of Bashan: for his mercy endureth for ever." Why, every singer as he sang those lines, which look to us like a mere repetition, must have felt how applicable they were to their present condition when there was a Moabite and an Edomite and an Ammonite to be overthrown in the name of the mighty God whose mercy endureth for ever. So they kept on singing.

You will observe that, while they were singing, God had wrought the great deliverance for them. When the singing ceased, *they prepared to gather up the spoil*. What a different employment from what they expected! You can see them stripping the bodies, taking off the helmet of gold and the greaves of brass; the jewels from the ears and from about the necks of the princes; spoiling the dead of their Babylonish garments and their wedges of gold; heaping up the tents—the rich tents of the eastern nations—till they said one to another, "We know not what to do." But the difficulty was different from what might have befallen them at the first. Then they did not know what to do because of their weakness in the presence of their foes, but now the difficulty was because of the greatness of the spoil. "We cannot carry it home," they would say to each other, "there is too much of it. It will take us days and days to stock away this wondrous booty." Now, child of God, it shall be so with you also. I do not know how, but if you can only trust God and praise him and go straight ahead, you shall see such wondrous things that you shall be utterly astonished.

Then what will you do? Why, you will at once again begin praising the Lord, for so they did. *They went back singing.* "They came back to Jerusalem with psalteries and harps and trumpets unto the house of the Lord." When God has done great things for you, and brought you through your present difficulty, you must be sure to repay him in the courts of his house with your loudest music and your most exultant notes, blessing again and again the name of the Lord.

After that *they had rest.* In the narrative it is added, "So the realm of Jehoshaphat was quiet: for his God gave him rest round about." His enemies were afraid to come and touch him any more. After a very sharp storm it generally happens that there is long rest. So shall it be with all the Lord's people. You will get through this trouble, brother, and afterwards it will be smooth sailing for a very long time. I have known a child of God have a very cyclone; it has seemed as if he must be utterly destroyed, but after it was over there has not been a ripple on the calm of his life. People have envied him and wondered at his quietness; he had had all his storms at once, and when they were over he had come into smooth water that seemed never ruffled. Perhaps you will have the same experience: only ask the great Pilot of the Galilean lake to steer you safely through your tempest, and then, when the storm shall cease at his bidding, you shall be glad because you be quiet; so will he bring you to your desired haven.

I have been desirous to speak these comfortable words to God's children, for well I know how they are tried, and I pray the Lord, the Comforter, to apply the word to their troubled hearts. But I never can finish my discourse without having the very sad thought that there are always in our congregation some to whom these comfortable things do not belong. They are not believers. They have never trusted in Christ. If this be so with you—if this be so —ah, friend, you have to fight your own battles: you have to bear your own trials, you have to carry your own burdens, and when you come at the last great day before the judgment seat you will have to answer for your own sins, and to bear your own punishment. God have mercy upon you, and deliver you from such a condition as this. It is a bad condition to live in; it is a terrible condition to die in. May you be brought to receive Christ for your substitute and your surety, and glorify his name for ever and ever. Amen.

11. A Wonderful Transformation

"Your sorrow shall be turned into joy."—John xvi. 20.

You all know that, at that time, our Lord was speaking of his death, which would cause the deepest grief to his own people, while the ungodly world would rejoice, and laugh them to scorn. So he bade them look beyond the immediate present into the future, and believe that, ultimately, the cause of their sorrow would become a fountain of perpetual joy to them. It is always well to look a little ahead. Instead of deploring the dark clouds, let us anticipate the fruits and the flowers that will follow the descent of the needed showers. We might be always wretched if we lived only in the present, for our brightest time is yet to come. We are now, as believers in the Lord Jesus Christ, only in the twilight of our day; the high noon shall come to us by-and-by.

But although our Saviour's words, just then, related immediately to his death, he was such a wonderful speaker that everything he said had a wider meaning in it than one might at first imagine. Even the leaves of the tree of life are for the healing of the nations; and even those words of Christ, which have a direct application to a special occasion, have a further wondrous power about them, and may be used on other occasions as well as upon the one when they were first uttered. I think I may fairly say that our Lord did not merely mean that, just when he died, his children would have sorrow; but that we may take his words as a prophecy that all who truly follow him will have their seasons of darkness and gloom. Our Lord Jesus Christ has nowhere promised to his people immunity from trial; on the contrary, he said to his disciples, " In the world ye shall have tribulation." I cannot imagine a better promise for the wheat than that it shall be threshed, and that is the promise that is made to us if we are the Lord's wheat, and not the enemy's tares, " Ye shall have the threshing which shall fit you for the

heavenly garner." You need not mourn, beloved, that it is to be
so; if you do, it will make no difference, for your Lord has
declared that "in the world ye shall have tribulation." Rest quite
sure of that. If you could ask those believers who are now in
heaven, they would tell you that they came there through great
tribulation; many of them not only washed their robes in the
blood of the Lamb, but they sealed their faithfulness to him with
their own blood.

Our Lord meant his disciples to feel the sorrow that was to
come upon them, for he said to them, "Ye shall weep and lament,"
and he did not express any blame upon them for doing so. I
would not have any of you imagine that there is any virtue in
stoicism. I once heard a woman, who wished to show the wonders
wrought in her by the grace of God, say that, when her babe was
taken from her, she was so resigned to the divine will that she did
not even shed a tear; but I do not believe that it ever was the
divine will that mothers should lose their babes without shedding
tears over them. I thank God that I did not have a mother who
could have acted like that; and I believe that, as Jesus himself
wept, there can be no virtue in our saying that we do not weep.
God means you to feel the rod, my brother, my sister. He intends
you sometimes to weep and lament, as Peter says, "if need be, ye
are in heaviness through manifold temptations." It is not merely
the temptation or trial for which there is a needs-be; but that we
should be in heaviness, is also a necessary part of our earthly
discipline. Unfelt trial is no trial; certainly, it would be an
unsanctified trial. Christ never meant Christians to be stoics.
There is a wide and grave distinction between a gracious acquiescence
in the divine will and a callous steeling of your heart to bear anything that happens without any feeling whatsoever. "Ye shall be
sorrowful," says our Lord to his disciples, and "ye shall weep and
lament." It is through the weeping and the lamenting, oftentimes,
that the very kernel of the blessing comes to us.

Our Saviour mentions one aggravation of our grief, which some of
us have often felt: "the world shall rejoice." That is the old story.
David found his own trials all the harder to bear when he saw
the prosperity of the wicked. He had been plagued all the day
long, and chastened every morning, and he could have endured
that if he had not seen that the ungodly had more than heart could
wish. He found himself, sometimes, even troubled with the fear
of death; but as for the wicked, he said, "There are no bands in
their death: but their strength is firm. They are not in trouble
as other men; neither are they plagued like other men." It makes
our bitterness all the more bitter when the saints of God are
afflicted, and the enemies of God are made to dwell at ease. I
daresay, when you were a boy, you may have fallen, and hurt
yourself; and while you were smarting from your bruises, the other
lads, who were round about you, were laughing at you. The pain
was all the sharper because of their laughing; and the righteous
are wounded to the quick when they see the ungodly prospering,—
prospering, apparently, by their ungodliness, and when these ungodly

persons point the finger of scorn at them, and ask, "Where is now your God? Is this the result of serving him?" When this is your lot, remember that your Saviour told his disciples that it would be so, and he has told you the same. While you are sorrowing, you shall hear their shouts of revelry. You shall be up in your own room weeping, and you shall hear the sound of their merry feet in the dizzy dance. The very contrast between their circumstances and your own will make you feel your grief the more. Well, if this is to be our lot, we must not count it a strange thing when it comes, but we may hear our Master say to us, "I told you that it would be so." When it happens to any of you, beloved, you also may say, "This is even as Jesus Christ said it would be." His first disciples, if they ventured out into the streets of Jerusalem after their Saviour's crucifixion, and while he was lying in the tomb of Joseph, must have found it very trying to hear the jests and jeers of those who had put the Nazarene to death. "There is an end of him now," they said; "his imposture is exposed, and his disciples, poor, foolish fanatics, will soon come to their senses now, and the whole thing will collapse." Just so; that was what Jesus said would happen, "Ye shall weep and lament, but the world shall rejoice."

Now, what was the Saviour's cure for all this? It was the fact that this trial was to last only for a little while,—for a very little while. In the case of his first disciples, it was only to last for a few days, and then it would be over, for they would hear the joyful announcement, "The Lord is risen indeed, and hath appeared to Simon." So is it to be with you and with me, dear brothers and sisters in Christ. Our sorrows are all, like ourselves, mortal. There are no immortal sorrows for immortal saints. They come; but, blessed be God, they also go. Like birds of the air, they fly over our heads; but they cannot make their abode in our souls. We suffer to-day, but we shall rejoice to-morrow. "Weeping may endure for a night, but joy cometh in the morning." But as for yonder laughing sinner, what weeping and wailing will be his portion unless he repents, and weeps in penitence over his many sins! The prosperity of the wicked is like a thin layer of ice on which they stand always in peril. In a moment, they may be brought down to destruction, and the place that knew them will know them no more for ever. Our weeping is soon to end; but their weeping will never end. Our joy will be for ever; but their joy will speedily come to an end. Look a little ahead, Christian pilgrims, for you will soon have passed through the valley of the shadow of death, and have come into the land where even the shadow of death shall never fall across your pathway again.

In speaking these comforting words to his disciples, our Saviour made use of this memorable sentence, "Your sorrow shall be turned into joy." As I read the whole passage, I pondered over those words, and tried to find out their meaning. Perhaps you think, as you glance at them, that they mean that the man who was sorrowful would be joyous. That is part of their meaning, but they mean a great deal more than that. They mean, literally and actually, your sorrow itself shall be turned into joy;—not the sorrow to be taken away, and joy to be put in its place, but the very sorrow, which now grieves you, shall be turned into joy. This is a very wonderful transformation; and only the God who worketh great marvels could possibly accomplish it;—could, somehow, not only take away the bitterness, and give sweetness in its place, but turn the bitterness itself into sweetness.

That is to be the subject of our present meditation; and I am glad to have, in the communion, at which many of us will presently unite in the highest act of Christian fellowship, an apt illustration of my theme. You know that the supper of the Lord is not at all a funereal gathering; but it is a sacred festival, at which we sit at our ease, restfully enjoying ourselves as at a banquet. But what are the provisions for this feast, and what do they represent? That bread, that wine,—what do they mean? They represent, my dear friends, sorrow,—sorrow even unto death. The bread, separate from the wine, represents the flesh of Christ separate from his blood, and so they set forth death. The broken bread represents the flesh of Christ bruised, marred, suffering, full of anguish. The wine represents Christ's blood poured out upon the cross, amidst agony which only ended with his death. Yet these emblems of sorrow and suffering furnish us with our great feast of love; this is indeed joy arising out of sorrow. The festival is itself the ordained memorial of the greatest grief that was ever endured on earth. Here, then, as you gather around this table, you shall see, in the outward sign and emblem, that sorrow is turned into joy.

I. If you will keep that picture in your mind's eye, it will help me to bring out the meaning of the text, and our first point will be this. OUR SORROW AS TO OUR BLESSED LORD IS NOW TURNED INTO JOY. The very things that make us grieve concerning him are the things which make us rejoice concerning him.

And, first, *this comes to pass when we look upon him as tempted, tried, and tested in a thousand ways.* We see him no sooner rising from the waters of baptism than he is led into the desert to be tempted of the devil, and we grieve to think that, for our sakes, it was needful that he should there bear the brunt of a fierce duel with the prince of darkness. We see him afterwards, all his life long, tempted, and tried, and tested, this way and that,—sometimes by a scribe or a Pharisee, sometimes by a Sadducee. All sorts of temptations were brought to bear upon him, for he "was in all points tempted like as we are." But, oh, how thankful we are to know that he was thus tempted, for those very temptations helped to prove the sinlessness of his character. How could we know what there was in a man who was never tested and tried? But our Lord was tested at every point, and at no point did he fail; it is established, beyond all question, that he is the Lamb of God without blemish and without spot. You cannot tell what a man's strength of character is unless he is tried; there must be something to develop the excellence that lies hidden in his nature; and we ought to rejoice and bless God that our Saviour was passed, like silver, through the furnace seven times; and, like gold, was tried again and again in the crucible, in the hottest part of the furnace, yet was there found no dross in him, but only the pure, precious metal, without a particle of alloy. Therein do we greatly rejoice. He "was in all points tempted like as we are, yet without sin;" he was assailed by Satan, and contradicted by sinners, yet he was found faultless to the end; and, thus, our joy arises out of that which otherwise would have made us mourn.

Further, dear brethren, remember that the griefs and trials of our Lord not only manifested his sinless character, but *they made him fit for that priestly office which he has undertaken on our behalf.* The Captain of our salvation was made "perfect through sufferings." It is needful that he, who would really be a benefactor to men, should know them thoroughly, and understand them. How can he sympathize with them in their sorrows unless he has, at least to some extent, felt as they do? So, our merciful and faithful High Priest is one who can be "touched with the feeling of our infirmities," seeing that he was tempted and tried even as we are. I think that, had I been alive at the time, I would have spared my Lord many of his griefs had it been in my power; and many of you will say the same. He should never have needed to say, "Foxes have holes, and birds of the air have nests; but the Son of man hath not where to lay his head," for you would gladly have given him the best room in your house. Ah, but then the poor would have missed that gracious word, which, I have no doubt, has often comforted them when they have been houseless and forlorn. You would not have allowed him, if you could have helped it, to be weary, and worn, and hungry, and thirsty. You would have liberally supplied all his wants to the utmost of your power; but, then, he would not have been so fully in sympathy as he now is with those who have to endure the direst straits of poverty, seeing that he has passed through a similar experience to theirs. What joy it is to a sorrowing soul to know that Jesus has gone that way long before! I had a great grief that struck me down to the very dust, but I looked up, and saw that face that was marred more than any other; and I rose to my feet in hope and joyful confidence, and I said, "Art thou, my Lord, here where I am? Hast thou suffered thus, and didst thou endure far more than I can ever know of grief and brokenness of heart? Then, Saviour, I rejoice, and bless thy holy name." I know that you, beloved, must often have grieved over your Saviour's suffering, though you have been, at the same time, glad to remember that he passed through it all, because he thus became such a matchless Comforter, "who can have compassion on the ignorant, and on them that are out of the way," because of the very experience through which he passed, "for in that he himself hath suffered being tempted, he is able to succour them that are tempted."

The meaning of the text comes out even more clearly when we think of *the sorrows to which our Lord had been referring, which ended in his death.* Oh, the griefs of Jesus when he laid down his life for his sheep! Have you not sometimes said, or at least thought, that the ransom price was too costly for such insignificant creatures as we are? Think of the agony and bloody sweat, the scourging, the spitting, the shame, the hounding through the streets, the piercing of the hands and feet, the mockery, the vinegar, the gall, the "Eloi Eloi, lama sabacthani?" and all the other horrors and terrors that gathered around the cross. We wish that they might never have happened; and yet the fact that they did happen brings to us bliss unspeakable. It is our greatest joy to know that Jesus bled and died upon the tree; how else could our sin be put away? How else could we, who are God's enemies, be reconciled and brought near to him? How else could heaven be made secure for us? We might, from one aspect of Christ's sufferings, chant a mournful *miserere* at the foot of the cross; but ere we have done more than just commence the sad strain, we perceive the blessed results that come to the children of men through Christ's death, so we lay down our instruments of mourning, and take up the harp and the trumpet, and sound forth glad notes of rejoicing and thanksgiving.

Our sorrow about Christ's death is also turned into joy because, not only do we derive the greatest possible benefit from it, but *Jesus himself, by his death, achieved such wonders.* That precious body of his—that fair lily all bestained with crimson lines, where flowed his heart's blood, must have been a piteous sight for anyone to see. I wonder how any artist could ever paint the taking down of Christ from the cross, or the robing him for the sepulchre. These were sorrowful sights for art to spend itself upon. Jesus, the final Conqueror, lies in the grave; the cerements of the tomb are wrapped about him who once wore the purple of the universe. But we have scarcely time to sorrow over these facts before we recollect that the death of Christ was the death of sin; the death of Christ was the overthrow of Satan; the death of Christ was the death of death; and out of his very tomb we hear that pealing trumpet-note, "O death, where is thy sting? O grave, where is thy victory? The sting of death is sin; and the strength of sin is the law. But thanks be to God, which giveth us the victory through our Lord Jesus Christ." I am glad that he fought with Satan in the garden, and vanquished him. I am glad that he fought with sin upon the cross, and destroyed it. I am glad that he fought with grim death in that dark hour, and that he seized him by the throat, and held him captive. I am glad that he ever entered the gloomy sepulchre, for he rifled it of all its terrors for all his loved ones, tore its iron bars away, and set his people free. So, you see, it is all gladness, even as he said to his disciples, "Your sorrow shall be turned into joy."

And whatever else there may be of sorrow that comes out of Christ's cross, we may all be glad of it, for, *now, Christ himself is the more glorious because of it.* It is true that nothing could add to his glory as God; but, seeing that he assumed our nature, and became man as well as God, he added to his glory by all the shame he bore. There is not a reproach that pierced his heart which did not make him more beautiful. There is not a line of sorrow that furrowed his face which did not make him more lovely; that marred countenance is more to be admired by us than all the comeliness of earthly beauty. He was ever superlatively beautiful; his beauty was such as might well hold the angels spellbound as they looked upon him. The sun and moon and stars were dim compared with the brightness of his eyes. Heaven and earth could not find his equal; and if all heaven had been sold, it could not have purchased this precious pearl; yet the setting of the pearl has made Christ appear even brighter than before,—the setting of his humanity, the setting of his sufferings, his pangs, his shameful death, has made his Deity shine out the more resplendent. The plant that sprang from Jesse's root is now the Plant of renown. He who was despised at Nazareth is glorified in Paradise, and the more glorified because, between Nazareth and Paradise, he was "despised and rejected of men, a man of sorrows, and acquainted with grief." Blessed Saviour, we rejoice that thou hast gained by all thy sorrows, for therefore hath God highly exalted thee, and given thee a name which is above every name.

II. But now, secondly, and very briefly, I want to remind you that THE SORROW OF THE WHOLE CHURCH HAS ALSO BEEN TURNED INTO JOY.

In speaking of *the sorrows of the persecuted Church of Christ*, I will not compare them to the sorrows of her Lord; but if anything could have been comparable to the suffering of the Bridegroom, it would have been the suffering of the bride. Think of the early ages of the Church of God, under the Roman persecutions. Think of the Church of Christ among the Vaudois of the Alps, or in England during the Marian persecution. Our blood runs cold as we read of what the saints of God have suffered, I have often put up Foxe's Book of Martyrs upon the shelf, and thought that I could not read it any more; it is such a terribly true account of what human nature can bear when faith in Christ sustains it. Yet, brethren, we are not sorry that the martyrs suffered as they did; or if we are, that very sorrow is turned into joy at the remembrance of how Christ has been glorified through the sufferings of his saints. Even our poor humanity looks more comely when we recall what it endured for Christ's sake. When I think of the honour of being a martyr for the truth, I confess that I would sooner be like him than be the angel Gabriel, for I think it would be far better to have gone to heaven from one of Smithfield's stakes than to have been always in heaven. What honour it has brought to Christ that poor, feeble men could love him so that they could bleed and die for him! Ay, and women too, like that brave Anne Askew, who, after they had racked her till they had put every bone out of joint, was still courageous enough to argue on behalf of her dear Lord; when they thought that her womanly weakness would make her give way, she seemed stronger than any man might have been as she said to her persecutors,—

> " I am not she that lyst
> My anker to let fall
> For every dryslynge myst ;
> My shippe's substancyal ;"—

and so defied them to do their worst. The Church of God may well rejoice as she thinks of the noble army of martyrs who praise the Lord on high; for, amongst the sweetest notes that ascend even in heaven, are the songs that come from the white-robed throng who shed their blood rather than deny their Lord.

The Church of Christ has also passed through a fierce fire of opposition, as well as of persecution. Heresy after heresy has raged, men have arisen who have denied this, and that, and the other doctrines taught in the Scriptures; and every time these oppositions have come, certain feeble folk in the Church have been greatly alarmed; but, in looking back upon them all up to the present, I think that they are causes for joy rather than sorrow. Whenever what is supposed to be a new heresy comes up, I say to myself, " Ah, I know you; I remember reading about you. There was an old pair of shoes, worn by heresy many hundreds of years ago, which were thrown on a dunghill; and you have picked them up, and vamped them a little, and brought them forth as if they had been new." I bless the Lord that, at this moment, there scarcely remains any doctrine to be defended for the first time, for they have all been fought over so fiercely in years gone by, that there is hardly any point that our noble forefathers did not defend; and they did their work so well that we can frequently use their weapons for the defence of the truth to-day. Who would wish to have kept the Word of God from going through this furnace of opposition? It is like silver seven times purified in a furnace of earth. Philosophers have tried thee, O precious Book; but thou wast not found wanting! Atheists have tried thee; sneering sceptics have tried thee; they have all passed thee through the fire, but not even the smell of fire is upon thee to this day; and therein do we rejoice, yea, and will rejoice. And the day will come when the present errors and opposition will only be recorded on the page of history as things for our successors to rejoice over just as we now rejoice over the past victories of the truth of God.

And once again, dear friends, not only is it so with the persecutions and oppositions of the Church of Christ, but *the Church's difficulties have also become themes of rejoicing.* As I look abroad upon the world at the present time, it does seem an impossible thing that the nations of the earth should ever be converted to Christ. It is impossible so far as man alone is concerned, yet God has commanded the Christian Church to evangelize the world. Someone complains that the Church is too feeble, and its adherents too few, to accomplish such a task as this. The fewer the fighters, the greater their share of glory when the victory is won. In order to overcome indifference, idolatry, atheism, Mohammedanism, and Popery, the battle must be a very stern one, but who wants Christ's followers to fight only little battles? My brethren and sisters, let us thank God that our foes are so numerous. It matters not how many there may be of them; there are only the more to be destroyed. What said David concerning his adversaries? " They compassed me about; yea, they compassed me about; but in the name of the Lord I will destroy them." When the last great day shall come, and Jehovah's banner shall be finally furled because the book of the wars of the Lord shall have reached its last page, it will be a grand thing to tell the story of the whole campaign. It will be known to all then that the fight for the faith was not a mere skirmish against a few feeble folk, nor was it a brief battle which began and ended in an hour; but it was a tremendous conflict "against principalities, against powers, against the rulers of the darkness of this world, against spiritual wickedness in high places." They gather, they gather, my brethren, thick as the clouds in the day of tempest, but out of heaven Jehovah himself will thunder, and give battle, and scatter them, and they shall fly before him like the chaff before the wind.

III. Now, lastly, to come down from those high themes to minor matters, OUR OWN PERSONAL SORROW SHALL BE TURNED INTO JOY.

When I think of the sorrows of Christ and the sorrows of his Church as a whole, I say to myself, "What pin-pricks are our griefs compared with the great gash in the Saviour's side, and the many scars that adorn his Church to-day!" But, dear friends, whatever our sorrows may be, they will be turned into joy. Sometimes we ourselves witness this wonderful transformation. Poor old Jacob sorrowed greatly when he thought that he had lost his favourite son Joseph. "An evil beast hath devoured him;" said he, "Joseph is without doubt rent in pieces;" and he wrung his hands, and wept bitterly for many a day over his lost Joseph. Then came the famine, and the poor old man was dreadfully alarmed concerning his large family. He must needs send some of his sons into Egypt to buy corn, and when he does send them there, they do not all come back, for Simeon is detained as a hostage, and the lord of the land says that they shall not see his face again unless they bring Benjamin with them,—Benjamin, the dear and only remaining child of the beloved Rachel. Jacob cannot bear the thought of parting with him, so he says to his sons, "Me have ye bereaved of my children; Joseph is not, and Simeon is not, and ye will take Benjamin away: all these things are against me." Poor old soul, what a mistake he made! Why, everything was as much for him as it could possibly be. There was his dear Joseph, down in Egypt, next to Pharaoh on the throne, and ready to provide for his poor old father and all the family during the time of famine. Then there was the famine to make him send down to Egypt, and find out where Joseph was, so that he might go and see his face again, and confess that the Lord had dealt graciously with him. You dear children of God, who get fretting and troubled, should carry out Cowper's good advice,—

"Judge not the Lord by feeble sense,
But trust him for his grace;
Behind a frowning providence
He hides a smiling face."

You have quite enough to cry over without fretting concerning things that, some day, you will rejoice over. The Lord will put your tears into his bottle, and when he shows them to you, by-and-

by, I think you will say, "How foolish I was ever to shed them, because the very thing I wept over was really a cause for rejoicing if I could but have seen a little way ahead." It is so sometimes, in providence, as you will find over and over again between here and heaven.

Our sorrows, dear friends, are turned into joy in many different ways. For instance, there are some of us, who are such naughty children, that *we never seem to come close to our Heavenly Father unless some sorrow drives us to him.* We ought to be more with him in days of sunshine, if it were possible, than in days of storm, but it is not always so. It is said that there are some dogs which, the more you whip them, the more they love you. I should not like to try that plan even on a dog; but I fear that some of us are very like dogs, in that respect, if the saying is true. When we have a great trouble, or get a sharp cut, we seem to wake up and say, "Lord, we forgot thee when all was going smoothly; we wandered from thee then, but now we must come back to thee." And there is a special softness of heart, and mellowness of spirit, which we often get through being tried and troubled; and when that is the case, you and I have great cause to rejoice in our sorrows, if they draw us nearer to God, and bring us to a closer and more careful walk with him. If they draw us away from worldliness, and self-sufficiency, and self-complacency, our sorrows, if we are wise men and women, will be immediately turned into joy.

Again, there is no doubt that, to many, *sorrow is a great means of opening the eyes to the preciousness of the promises of God.* I believe that there are some of God's promises, of which we shall never get to know the meaning until we have been placed in the circumstances for which those promises were written. Certain objects in nature can only be seen from certain points of view, and there are precious things in the covenant of grace that can only be perceived from the deep places of trouble. Well, then, if your trouble brings you into a position where you can understand more of the lovingkindness of the Lord, you may be very thankful that you were ever put there, and may thus find your sorrow turned into joy.

Again, *sorrow often gives us further fellowship with Christ.* There are times when we can say, "Now, Lord, we can sympathize with thee better than we ever did before, for we have felt somewhat as thou didst in thine agony here below." We have sometimes felt as though that prophecy had been fulfilled to us, "Ye shall drink indeed of my cup, and be baptized with the baptism that I am baptized with." For instance, if friends forsake you,—if he that eateth bread with you lifteth up his heel against you, you can say, "Now, Lord, I know a little better what thy feeling was when Judas so basely betrayed thee." You cannot so fully comprehend the griefs of Christ unless, in your humble measure, you have to pass through a somewhat similar experience; but when you perceive that you can sympathize more with Christ because of your own sorrow, then, for certain, your sorrow is turned into joy.

Sorrow also gives us fellowship with our Lord in another way,—

when we feel as if Christ and we had become partners in one trouble. Here is a cross, and I have to carry one end of it; but I look round, and see that my Lord is carrying the heavier end of it, and then it is a very sweet sorrow to carry the cross in partnership with Christ. Rutherford says, in one of his letters, "When Christ's dear child is carrying a burden, it often happens that Christ saith, 'Halves, my love,' and carries the half of it for him." It is indeed sweet when it is so. If there be a ring of fire on your finger, and that ring means that you are married to Christ, you may well be willing to wear it, whatever suffering it may cause you. Those were blessed bolts that fastened you to the cross, even though they were bolts of iron that went right through your flesh, for they kept you the more closely to your Lord. Our motto must be, "Anywhere with Jesus; nowhere without Jesus." Anywhere with Jesus; ay, even in Nebuchadnezzar's furnace, when we have the Son of God with us, the glowing coals cannot hurt us, they become a bed of roses to us when he is there. Where Jesus is, our sorrow is turned into joy.

I must not fail to remind you that there is a time coming when "the sorrows of death" will get hold upon us; and I want you, brethren and sisters, to understand that, unless the Lord shall come first, *we shall not escape the sorrow of dying, but it will be turned into joy.* It has been my great joy to see many Christians in their last moments on earth, and I am sure that the merriest people I have ever seen have been dying saints. I have been to wedding feasts; I have seen the joy of young people in their youth; I have seen the joy of the merchant when he has made a prosperous venture; and I have myself experienced joys of various kinds; but I have never seen any joy that I have so envied as that which has sparkled in the eyes of departing believers. There rises up before me now a vision of the two eyes of a poor consumptive girl,—oh, how bright they were! I heard that she must soon die, so I went to try to comfort her. To comfort her? Oh, dear, she needed no comforting from me! Every now and then, she would burst forth into a verse of sacred song; and when she stopped, she would tell me how precious Jesus was to her, what love visits he had already paid her, and how soon she expected to be for ever with him. There was not, in all the palaces of Europe, or in all the mansions of the wealthy, or in all the ball-rooms of the gay, such a merry and joyous spirit as I saw shining through the bright eyes of that poor consumptive girl, who had very little here below, but who had so much laid up for her in heaven that it did not matter what she had here. Yes, beloved, your sorrow will be turned into joy. Many of you will not even know that you are dying; you will shut your eyes on earth, and open them in heaven. Some of you may be dreading death, for there is still a measure of unbelief remaining in you; but, in your case also, death will be swallowed up in victory. Just as, when some people have to take physic which is very bitter, it is put into some sweet liquid, and they drink it down without tasting the bitterness, so will it be with all of us who are trusting in the Lord Jesus Christ when we have to drink our last potion. In a few more days, or weeks, or months, or years,—it does not matter which, for it will be a very short time at the longest,—all of us who love the Lord will be with him where he is, to behold his glory, and to share it with him for ever. Have any of you any sorrows that you still wish to talk about? Some of you are very poor, and others of you are very much tried and troubled in many ways; but, my dear friends, when you and I get up there,—and we shall do so before long,—I think you will have the best of it. If there is any truth in that line,—

"The deeper their sorrows, the louder they'll sing,"—

the more sorrows you have had, the more will you sing. Nobody enjoys wealth like a man who has been poor. Nobody enjoys health like a man who has been sick. I think that the pleasantest days I ever spend are those that follow a long illness, when I at last begin to creep out of doors, and drink in the sweet fresh air again. And, oh, what joy it will be to you poor ones, and you sick ones, and you tried ones, to get into the land where all is plentiful, where all is peaceful, where all is gladsome, where all is holy! You will be there soon,—some of you will be there very soon. Dr. Watts says that—

> "There, on a green and flowery mount,
> Our weary souls shall sit,
> And with transporting joys recount
> The labours of our feet."

That is to say, the very sorrows that we pass through in our earthly pilgrimage, will constitute topics for joyful converse in heaven. I do not doubt that it will be so. In heaven, we shall be as glad of our troubles as of our mercies. Perhaps it will appear to us, then, that God never loved us so much as when he chastened and tried us. When we get home to glory, we shall be like children who have grown up, who sometimes say to a wise parent, "Father, I have forgotten about the holidays you gave me; I have forgotten about the pocket money you gave; I have forgotten about a great many sweet things that I very much liked when I was a child; but I have never forgotten that whipping which you gave me when I did wrong, for it saved me from turning altogether aside. Dear father, I know you did not like to do it, but I am very grateful to you for it now,—more grateful for that whipping than for all the sponge-cakes and sweetmeats that you gave me." And, in like manner, when we get home to heaven, I have no doubt that we shall feel, and perhaps say, "Lord, we are grateful to thee for everything, but most of all for our sorrows. We see that, hadst thou left us unchastized, we should never have been what we now are; and, thus, our sorrows are turned into joy."

As for you who are not believers in the Lord Jesus Christ, I want you to ponder most solemnly these few words, and carry them home with you. *If you remain as you are, your joys will be turned into sorrows.* God grant that they may not be, for Jesus Christ's sake! Amen.

12. A Harp of Ten Strings

"And Mary said, My soul doth magnify the Lord, and my spirit hath rejoiced in God my Saviour."—Luke i. 46, 47.

It is very clear that Mary was not beginning a new thing; for she speaks in the present tense, and in a tense which seems to have been for a long time present : "My soul doth magnify the Lord." Ever since she had received the wonderful tidings of the choice which God had made of her for her high position, she had begun to magnify the Lord; and when once a soul has a deep sense of God's mercy, and begins magnifying him, there is no end to it. This grows by what it feeds upon : the more you magnify God, the more you can magnify him. The higher you rise, the more you can see; your view of God is increased in extent; and whereas you praised him somewhat at the bottom of the hill, when you get nearer and nearer to the top of his exceeding goodness, you lift up the strain still more loudly, and your soul doth more fully and exultantly magnify the Lord.

"My soul doth magnify the Lord." What does it mean ? The usual signification of the word "magnify" is, to make great, or to make to appear great. We say, when we use the microscope, that it magnifies so many times. The insect is the same small and tiny thing; but it is increased to our apprehension. The word is very suitable in this connection. We cannot make God greater than he is. Nor can we have any conception of his actual greatness. He is infinitely above our highest thoughts; when we meditate upon his attributes—

> "Imagination's utmost stretch
> In wonder dies away."

But we magnify him by having higher, larger, truer conceptions of him; by making known his mighty acts, and praising his glorious name, so that others, too, may exalt him in their thoughts. This is what Mary was doing : she was a woman who was given, in after-life, to pondering. Those who heard what the shepherds said concerning the holy child Jesus wondered; but "Mary kept all these things, and pondered them in her heart." They wondered; Mary pondered. It is only the change of a letter; but it makes a great difference in the attitude of the soul, a change from a vague flash of interest to a deep attention of heart. She pondered; she weighed the matter; she turned it over in her mind; she thought about it; she estimated its value and result. She was like that other Mary, a meditative woman, who could quietly wait at her Lord's feet to hear gracious words, and drink them in with yearning faith.

It is no idle occupation thus to get alone, and in your own hearts to magnify the Lord; to make him great to your mind, to your affections; great in your memory, great in your expectations. It is one of the grandest exercises of the renewed nature. You need not, at such a time, think of the deep questions of Scripture, and may leave the abstruse doctrines to wiser heads, if you will; but if your very soul is bent on making God great to your own apprehension, you will be spending time in one of the most profitable ways possible to a child of God. Depend upon it, there are countless holy influences which flow from the habitual maintenance of great thoughts of God, as there are incalculable mischiefs which flow from our small thoughts of him. The root of false theology is belittling God; and the essence of true divinity is greatening God, magnifying him, and enlarging our conceptions of his majesty and his glory to the utmost degree.

But Mary did not mean, by magnifying the Lord, merely to extol him in her own thoughts; being a true poetess, she intended to magnify the Lord by her words. No, I must correct myself; she did not *intend* to do it, she had been doing it all along, she was doing it when she came, panting and breathless, into her cousin Elizabeth's house. She said, "My soul doth magnify the Lord. I am now in such a favoured condition that I cannot open my mouth to talk to you, Elizabeth, without speaking of my Lord. My soul now seems filled with thoughts of him. I must speak, first of all, about *him*, and say such things of his grace and power as may help even you, my goodly elder sister, still to think grander thoughts of God than you have ever before enjoyed. My soul doth magnify the Lord."

We must recall the fact that Mary was highly distinguished and honoured. No other woman was ever blessed as she was; perhaps no other could have borne the honour that was put upon her—to be the mother of the human nature of our Saviour. It was the highest possible honour that could be put upon mortal, and the Lord knew, at the appointed time, where to find a guileless, lowly woman, who could be entrusted with such a gift, and yet not seek to filch away his glory. She is not proud; nay, it is a false heart that steals the revenues of God, and buys therewith the intoxicating cup of self-congratulation. The more God gives to a true heart, the more it gives to him. Like Peter's boat, which sank into the waters the more deeply, the more fully it was laden with fish, God's true children sink in their own esteem, as they are honoured by their Lord. God's gifts, when he gives grace with them, do not puff us up; they build us up. A humble and lowly estimate of ourselves is added to a greater esteem of him. The more God gives thee, the more do thou magnify him, and not thyself. Be this thy rule—" He must increase, but I must decrease."

Be thou less and less. Be thou the Lord's humble handmaid, yet bold and confident in thy praise of him who hath done for thee great things. Henceforth and for ever, let this be the one description of thy life: "My soul doth magnify the Lord; I have nothing else to do any more but to magnify him, and to rejoice in God my Saviour."

A week might be profitably employed were I to attempt to preach upon each part of Mary's song; but with quite another purpose in view, I am going to present it to you as a whole. As I put before you this instrument of ten strings, I will ask you, just for a minute or two, to place your fingers on each of them as they shall be indicated, and see whether you cannot wake some melody to the praise of the great King, some harmony in his honour; whether you cannot, at this good hour, magnify the Lord, and rejoice in God your Saviour. Luther used to say that the glory of Scripture was to be found in the pronouns; and it is certainly true of the text. Look at the personal touch of them, how it comes over and over again! "*My* soul doth magnify the Lord, and *my* spirit hath rejoiced in God *my* Saviour." At one of our Orphanage Festivals, I put before our many friends who were gathered together several reasons why everybody should contribute to the support of the children; indeed, I said, nobody ought to go off the ground without giving something. I was struck with one brother, who had no money with him, but who brought me his watch and chain. "Oh," I said, "do not give me them; these things sell for so little compared with their value;" but he insisted upon my keeping them, and said, "I will redeem them to-morrow, but I cannot go away without giving something now." How glad I would be if every child of God here should be as earnest in adoration, and say, "I am going to give some praise to God at this service: out of some of those strings I will get music; perhaps out of them all. I will endeavour with my whole heart to say, at some portion of the sermon, and from some point of view, 'My soul doth magnify the Lord'!" Do I hear you whisper, "My soul is very heavy"? Lift it up, then, by praising the Lord; begin a psalm, even if at first the tune must be in a minor key: soon the strain will change, and the "Miserere" become a "Hallelujah Chorus."

I. The first string which Mary seems to touch, and which, I trust, we, too, may reach with the hand of faith, is that of THE GREAT JOY WHICH THERE IS IN THE LORD. "My soul doth magnify the Lord, and my spirit hath rejoiced in God my Saviour." Let us bless God that our religion is not one of gloom. I do not know of any command anywhere in Scripture, "Groan in the Lord alway; and again I say, Groan." From the conduct of some people, we might almost imagine that they must have altered their New Testament in that particular passage, and thus wofully changed the glory of the original verse, "Rejoice in the Lord alway: and again I say, Rejoice." The first I ever knew of Christ my Master truly, was when I found myself at the foot of his cross, with the great burden that had crushed me effectually gone. I looked round for it, wondering where it could be, and, behold, it was tumbling down into his sepulchre! I have never seen it since, blessed be his name, nor do I ever want to see it again! Well do I remember the leaps I gave for joy when first I found that

all my burden of guilt had been borne by him, and was now buried
in the depths of his grave.

> "Many days have passed since then ;
> Many changes I have seen ! "

I have been to a great many wells to draw water ; but when I have
drawn it, and tasted thereof, it has been brackish as the waters of
Marah ; but whenever I have gone to this well—"my God, my
Saviour "—I have never drawn one drop that was not sweet and
refreshing. He who truly knows God must be glad in him ; to abide
in his house is to be still praising him ; yea, we may exult in him all
the day long. A very notable word is that which is found in the mouth
of David : " God my exceeding joy." Other things may give us
pleasure ; we may be happy in the gifts of God, and in his creatures ,
but God himself, the spring of all our joys, is greater than them all.
Therefore, " Delight thyself also in the Lord." This is his command ;
and is it not a lovely one? Let no one say that the faith of the Christian
is not to be exultant ; it is to be a delight ; and so greatly does God
desire us to rejoice in him, that to the command is added a promise,
"And he shall give thee the desires of thine heart." What a religion
is ours, in which delight becomes a duty, in which to be happy is to be
obedient to a command ! Heathen religions exact not only self-denials
of a proper kind, but tortures which men invent to accustom themselves to misery ; but in our holy faith, if we keep close to Christ, while
it is true that we bear the cross, it is also true that the cross ceases to
be a torture ; in fact, it often bears us as we bear it ; we discover in
the service of our Master that " his yoke is easy, and his burden is
light," and, strange to say, his burden gives us rest, and his yoke
gives us liberty. We have never had anything from our Master but
it has ultimately tended to our joy. Even when his rod has made us
smart he has intended it to work for our good, and so has it wrought.
Praise him, then, for such goodness.

Our religion is one of holy joy, especially with regard to our
Saviour. The more we understand that glorious word " Saviour",
the more are we ready to dance with delight. " My spirit hath rejoiced
in God *my Saviour*." The good tidings of great joy have reached us,
and as we, by his grace, have believed them, he has saved us from
sin, and death, and hell. He has not simply promised to do it some
day, but he has done it ; we have been saved. What is more, we
have, many of us, entered into rest by faith in him ; salvation is to us
a present experience at this hour, though we still wait for the fulness
of it to be revealed in the world to come.

Oh, come, let us joy in our Saviour ! Let us thank him that we have
so much for which to thank him. Let us praise him that there is so
much that we may rejoice in ; nay, so much that we must rejoice in.
Let us adore his dear name that he has so arranged the whole plan of
salvation, that it is calculated to bring heaven to us while we are here,
and to bring us who are here into heaven hereafter. Thus we lift up
our hearts because of the great joy there is laid up for us in God.
This is the first string : touch it now ; think of all the joy you have
had in God ; praise him for all the holy mirth he has given you in

his house; the bliss of communion with him at his table; the delights of fellowship with him in secret. Sing to him with a grateful heart, saying, "My soul doth magnify the Lord."

II. The second string we would desire to lay our fingers upon is THE GODHEAD OF OUR SAVIOUR. "My soul doth magnify the Lord." I have not a little Lord. "And my spirit hath rejoiced in *God my Saviour*." I know that my Saviour is a man, and rejoice in his humanity; but we will contend to the death for this—that he is more than man; he is our Saviour. One human being could not redeem another, or give to God a ransom for his brother. An angel's arm could not bear the tremendous load of the disaster of the Fall; but Christ's arm is more than angelic. He whom we magnify as our Saviour counted it not robbery to be equal with God; and when he undertook the wondrous task of our redemption, he brought the Godhead with him to sustain him in the more than herculean labour. Our trust is in Jesus Christ, very God of very God; we shall never cease, not only to believe in him, but to speak of him, and rejoice in him, and sing of him, as the incarnate Deity. What a frozen religion that is which has not the Godhead of Christ in it! Surely, they must be men of a very sanguine and imaginative temperament who can pretend to receive any comfort out of a Christianity which has not the divine Saviour as its very centre. I would as soon think of going to an iceberg to warm myself, as to a faith of that kind to find comfort. Nobody can ever praise up Christ too much for you and for me; they can never say too much of his wisdom, or of his power. Every divine attribute ascribed to Christ makes us lift up a new song unto him; for, whatever he may be to others, he is to us God over all, blessed for ever. Amen.

I wish that I could sing instead of speaking to you of him who was with the Father before all worlds began, whose delights, even then, were with the sons of men in prospect of their creation. I wish that I could tell the wonderful story of how he entered into covenant with God on the behalf of his people; and pledged himself to pay the debts of those his Father gave to him. He undertook to gather into one fold all the sheep whom he pledged himself to purchase with his precious blood; he engaged to bring them back from all their wanderings, and fold them on the hill-tops of the Delectable Mountains at his Father's feet. This he vowed to do; and he has gone about his task with a zeal that clothed him as a cloak; and he will achieve the divine purpose before he delivers up the kingdom to God, even the Father. "He shall not fail nor be discouraged." It is our delight to hear this Son of God, this Son of Mary, this wondrous Being in his complex nature as our Mediator, exalted and extolled, and made very high. Have you not sometimes felt that if the minister preached more about Jesus Christ, you would be very glad to hear him? I hope that is your inclination; yet I am afraid that we talk a great deal about many things rather than about our Master. Come, let me hear of him; sing to me or talk to me of Jesus, whose name is honey in the mouth, and music in the ear, and heaven in the heart. Oh, for more praise to his holy name! Yes, some of us can touch this string, and say with Mary, "My soul doth magnify the Lord, and my spirit hath rejoiced in God my Saviour."

III. The third string has softer, sweeter music in it, and it may suit some of us better than the sublimer themes that we have touched already. Let us sing, and magnify the LORD's LOVING CONDESCENSION ; for so the blessed virgin did when she went on to say, " for he hath regarded the low estate of his handmaiden." Here is something to sing about ; for ours was not only a low estate, but perhaps some here would have had to say, like Gideon, " My family is poor, and I am the least in my father's house," and, like him, you would have been passed over by most of the people. Perhaps even in your own family you were counted as nobody ; if there was a jest uttered, you were sure to be the butt of it, and generally you were misunderstood, and your actions misinterpreted. This was a trying experience for you ; but from this you have been gloriously delivered. It may have been that, like Joseph, you were a little dreamy, and perhaps you were a trifle too fond of telling your dreams. Yet, though because of this you were much put upon, the Lord at length raised up your head above those round about you. It may have been that your lot in life was cast among the very poorest and lowest of mankind ; yet the Lord has looked upon you in infinite compassion, and saved you. Will you not, then, magnify him ?

If Christ wanted a people, why did he not choose the kings, and princes, and nobles of the earth ? Instead of that, he takes the poor, and makes them to know the wonders of his dying love ; and instead of selecting the wisest men in the world, he takes even the most foolish, and instructs them in the things of the kingdom.

> " Wonders of grace to God belong,
> Repeat his mercies in your song."

All of us who have been saved by grace must strike a tenderer note still ; for we were sinful as well as lowly. We went astray like lost sheep ; therefore we magnify the Lord, who bought us, and sought us, and brought us back to his fold. It may be painful to remember what we once were, but it is well sometimes to go back in our thoughts to the time past when we lived in sin, that we may the better appreciate the favour of which we have been made partakers. When the apostle Paul wrote out a catalogue of those who shall not inherit the kingdom of God, he added, "And such were some of you : but ye are washed." Oh, let us bless the name of the Lord, and magnify him for this ! Who else could have cleansed us from our sin, or in what other fountain save that opened to the house of David could we have plunged, to rid us of our awful defilement ? He stoops very low, for some of God's elect were once the offscouring of all things ; and even when converted, many of them remained so in the estimate of the world, which sneers at humble Christians. If the professed followers of Christ happen to meet in some fine building, and worship God with grand music and gorgeous ritual, then the people of the world put up with them ; they may go even so far as to patronize them, though, even then, their respect is chiefly called forth, not on behalf of the people, but because of the building, the fine music, and the carriages. The carriages are especially important, for without a certain number of them at the door, it is deemed impossible to have a proper display of cultured Christianity. But the more God's people cling to the Lord, the less likely are they to be esteemed by the vulgar judgment of unholy men. Yet the Lord has chosen such, blessed be his name! It is a great wonder to me that the Lord ever chose some of you; but it is a far greater wonder that he should ever have chosen me. I can somehow understand his love of you, when I look at the gracious points in your character, though I am fully aware that they are only wrought by grace; but I cannot understand the love which he has displayed to me, who am the least of all the saints. "Oh!" say you, "that is what we were going to say about ourselves." Yes, I know. I am trying to put it into your mouths, so that we may all join in adoring gratitude. It is a miracle of mercy that he should have loved any of us, or stooped in his grace to have raised such beggars from the dunghill to set us among the princes at his right hand.

> "Why was I made to hear thy voice,
>   And enter while there's room ;
> When thousands make a wretched choice,
>   And rather starve than come?"

IV. The next string, however, is THE GREATNESS OF GOD'S GOOD-NESS; for Mary goes on to sing,—"He hath regarded the low estate of his handmaiden: for, behold, from henceforth all generations shall call me blessed." Oh, the Lord has done great things for his people! "He that is mighty hath done to me great things; and holy is his name." God has made you blessed. You were once under the curse, but for you there is now no condemnation, for you are in Christ Jesus. If the curse had withered you, like some lightning-blasted oak, you could not have wondered; but, instead thereof, the gracious Lord has planted you by the rivers of water, and he makes you to bring forth your fruit in your season, and your leaf also doth not wither. "The Lord hath done great things for us; whereof we are glad." To be lifted up from that horrible pit is such a great thing that we cannot measure it, but to be set up on that throne of mercy exceeds our highest thought: who can measure that? Take your line, and see if you can fathom the depth of such grace, or measure the height of such mercy. Shall we be silent when we behold such marvellous loving-kindness? God forbid it! Let us break forth in our hearts now with gladsome hallelujahs to him who has done such wonderful things for us!

Think, brethren, you were blind: he has made you see. You were lame: he has made you leap. Worse than that, you were dead: he has made you live. You were in prison : and he has made you free. Some of us were in the dungeon, with our feet fast in the stocks. Can I not well remember when I did lie in that inner prison, moaning and groaning, without any voice to comfort me, or even a ray of light to cheer me in the darkness? And now that he has brought me out, shall I forget to utter my deep thanks? Nay, but I will sing a song of deliverance, that others may hear, and fear, and turn unto the Lord. But that is not all. He has not only taken us from the prison, he has raised us to the throne : you and I could go in and out of heaven to-night, if God called us there, and every angel would treat us with respect. If we entered into the glory-land, even though we had come from the poorest home in London, we should find that the highest angels are only ministering servants to the chosen people of God. Oh, he has done wonders for us!

I am not so much attempting to preach, as trying to wake up your memory, that you may think of the goodness of the Lord's grace, and say, "Oh, yes, it is so, and my soul doth magnify the Lord!" Not one of the wonders of divine grace has been wrought for us without deep necessity for its manifestation. If the very least grace, which may perhaps hitherto have escaped your attention, were taken from you, where would you be? I often meet with people of God who used to be very happy and joyful, but who have fallen into despondency, and who now talk about the mercies of God's covenant love in such a way as to make me blush. They say, "I thought I once had that blessing, sir, and I am afraid I have not got it now, though there is nothing I long for more. Oh, what a precious thing it would be to be able to have access to God in prayer! I would give my eyes to be able to know that I am really a child of God." Yet those of us who have these blessings do not half value them; nay, brethren, we do not value them a thousandth part as much as we ought. Our constant song should be, "Blessed be the Lord, who daily loadeth us with benefits, even the God of our salvation." Instead of that, we often take the gifts thoughtlessly and unthankfully from his hand. When a man is in the sea, he may have much water over his head and not feel it; but when he comes out, if you then put a little pail of water on his head, it becomes quite a burden as he carries it. So some of you are swimming in God's mercy; you are diving into it, and you do not recognize the weight of the glory which God hath bestowed upon you; but if you should once get out of this ocean of joy, and fall into a state of sadness of heart, you would begin to appreciate the weight of any one of the mercies which now do not seem to be of much consequence, or to make any claim upon your gratitude. Without waiting to lose the sense of God's grace, in order that we may know the value of it, let us bless him who has done such inconceivably great things for us, and say, "My soul doth magnify the Lord."

V. The fifth string that I would touch is THE COMBINATION OF GRACE AND HOLINESS that there is in what God has done for us. "He that is mighty hath done to me great things; and holy is his name." I may not even hint at the peculiar delicacy of Mary's case, but she knew that it was wholly holy and pure. Now, when the Lord has saved you and me, who did not deserve saving, he did a very wonderful act of sovereign grace in making us to differ, but the mercy is that he did it all justly. Nobody can say that it ought not to be done. At the last great day, what God has done in his grace will stand the test of justice; for he has never, in the splendour and lavishness of his love, violated the principles of eternal righteousness, even to save his own elect. "He that is mighty hath done to me great things; and holy is his name." Sin must be punished: it has been punished in the person of our glorious Substitute. No man can enter into heaven unless he is perfectly pure: they who are redeemed shall take no unclean thing within the gates. Every rule and mandate of the divine empire shall be observed. The Law-maker will not be the law-breaker even to save the sinner; but his law shall be honoured as surely as the sinner shall be saved. Sometimes I feel that I could play on that string for an hour or two. Here we have justice magnified in grace, and holiness rejoicing in the salvation of sinners. The attributes of God are like the terrible crystal shining out with its clear white light, which yet may be divided into all the colours of the prism; each different, and all beautiful. The dazzling radiance of God is too glorious for our mortal eyes, but each revelation teaches us more of his beauty and perfectness. In the ruby light of an atoning sacrifice we are enabled to see how God is just and yet the Justifier of him that believeth in Jesus. Glory be to his name for the power of grace mingled with holiness! My soul doth magnify the Lord for this wonderful salvation, in which every attribute shall have its glory; justice as well as mercy, wisdom as well as might. "Mercy and truth are met together; righteousness and peace have kissed each other." Who could have invented such a plan, and who could have carried it out when it was thought of? Only he who came " with dyed garments from Bozrah." "My soul doth magnify the Lord, and my spirit hath rejoiced in God my Saviour."

VI. The sixth string is one which should be sweet every way. Mary now goes on to touch the string of GOD'S MERCY. "And his mercy is on them that fear him." The saints of old often touched this string in the temple. They often sang it, lifting up the refrain again and again—" His mercy endureth for ever ! "

> " For his mercy shall endure,
> Ever faithful, ever sure."

Mercy! Sinner, this is the silver bell for you: it is of the Lord's mercies that you are not consumed, because his compassions fail not. Listen to the heavenly music that calls you to repent and live. God delighteth in mercy. He waiteth to be gracious. Mercy! Saint, this is the golden bell for you; for you need mercy still. Standing with your foot upon the jasper doorstep of Paradise, with the pearly gate just before you, you will still need mercy to help you over the last step; and when you enter the choir of the redeemed, mercy shall be your perpetual song. In heaven you will chant the praises of the God of grace, whose mercy endureth for ever.

Do you mourn over your own backslidings? God will have mercy upon thee, dear child, though thou hast wandered since thou hast known him. Come back to him this very hour. He would woo thee again. He would press thee to his bosom. Hast thou not often been restored, hast thou not often had thy iniquities put away from thee in the years gone by? If so, again this moment touch thou this string—a child's finger can make it bring forth its music—touch it now. Say, "Yes, concerning mercy, mercy to the very chief of sinners, my soul doth magnify the Lord, and my spirit hath rejoiced in God my Saviour."

VII. Time would fail us if we tried to dwell at any length upon these wondrous themes; so we pass to the next string, number seven,

God's immutability, because in the verse we have already touched upon, there are two notes. Mary said, "His mercy is on them that fear him from generation to generation." He that had mercy in the days of Mary, has mercy to-day: "from generation to generation." He is the same God. "I am the Lord, I change not; therefore ye sons of Jacob are not consumed." You that once delighted in the Lord, do not suppose that he has altered. He still invites you to come and delight in him. He is "Jesus Christ the same yesterday, and to-day, and for ever." What a poor foundation we should have for our hope if God could change! But he has confirmed his word by an oath "that by two immutable things, in which it was impossible for God to lie, we might have a strong consolation, who have fled for refuge to lay hold upon the hope set before us." The God of my grandfather, the God of my father, is my God this day; the God of Abraham, Isaac, and Jacob is the God of every believer; he is the same God, and is prepared to do the same, and to be the same to us as to them. Look back into your own experience; have you not found God always the same? Come, protest against him, if you have ever found him to change. Is the mercy-seat altered? Do the promises of God fail? Has God forgotten to be gracious? Will he be favourable no more? Ay, even "if we believe not, yet he abideth faithful: he cannot deny himself;" and when all things else melt away, this one eternal rock abides; therefore, "My soul doth magnify the Lord, and my spirit hath rejoiced in God my Saviour." It is a blessed string to touch. If we had time, we would play upon it, and evoke such harmonies as would make the angels want to join us in the chorus.

VIII. The next string which will awaken a responsive echo in your hearts is God's power. "He hath shewed strength with his arm; he hath scattered the proud in the imagination of their hearts." This string gives us deep bass music, and requires a heavy hand to make it pour forth any melody. What wonders of power God has wrought on the behalf of his people, from the days of Egypt, when the horse and his rider he cast into the Red Sea, even till now! How strong is his arm to defend his people! In these days some of us have been driven to look to that power, for all other help has failed. You know how it was in the dark ages: it seemed as if the darkness of popery could never be removed; but how soon it was gone when God called forth his men to bear witness to his Son! What reason we have to rejoice that he "scattered the proud in the imagination of their hearts"! They thought that they could readily burn up the heretics, and put an end to this gospel of theirs; but they could not do it. And to-day there is a dark conspiracy to stamp out the evangelical faith. First, on the part of some who go after their superstitions, set up the crucifix to hide the cross, and point men to sacraments instead of to the Saviour. And then, worse than these, are those who undermine our faith in Holy Scripture, tear from the Book this chapter and that, deny this great truth and the other, and try to bring the inventions of man into the place that ought to be occupied by the truth of God. But the Lord liveth: Jehovah's arm hath not waxed short. Depend upon it, ere many years have passed, he will take up the quarrel of his covenant, and will bring the old banner to the front again. We shall yet

rejoice to hear the gospel preached in plainest terms, accentuated by
the Holy Ghost himself upon the hearts of his people. Let us touch
this string again. The Almighty God is not dead. "Behold, the
Lord's hand is not shortened, that it cannot save; neither his ear
heavy, that it cannot hear."

IX. The next string is one that some friends do not like; at least,
they do not say much about it: it is DIVINE SOVEREIGNTY. Listen to
it. You know how God thunders it out. "I will have mercy on
whom I will have mercy, and I will have compassion on whom I will
have compassion." God's will is supreme. Whatever the wills of
men may be, God will not be driven from the throne, nor will his
sceptre be made to quiver in his hands; after all the rebellious acts
of men and devils, he will be still eternal and supreme, with his kingdom ruling over all. And thus the virgin sings, "He hath put down
the mighty from their seats, and exalted them of low degree. He hath
filled the hungry with good things; and the rich he hath sent empty
away." Who can speak the wonders of his sovereign grace? Was
it not strange that he should ever have chosen you?

> " What was there in you that could merit esteem,
>   Or give the Creator delight ?
> "'Twas even so, Father,' you ever must sing,
>   ' Because it seem'd good in thy sight.' "

Is it not strange that the Lord should not take the kings and
mighty ones, but should so order it, that the poor have the gospel
preached to them? God is King of kings, and Lord of lords; and he
acts like a king. "He giveth not account of any of his matters." But
he lets us see right clearly that he has no respect to the greatness
and fancied goodness of man; that he does as he pleases; and that he
pleases to give his mercy to them that fear him, and bow before him.
He dispenses his favours to those who tremble at his presence, who
come humbly to his feet, and take his mercy as a free gift; who
look to his dear Son because they have nothing else to look to, and, as
poor, guilty worms, find in Christ their life, their wisdom, their
righteousness, their all. Oh, the splendour of this great King !

X. The tenth string is GOD'S FAITHFULNESS. "He hath holpen
his servant Israel, in remembrance of his mercy; as he spake to our
fathers, to Abraham, and to his seed for ever." God remembers what
he has said. Take those three words, "As he spake." Whatever
he said, though it be thousands of years ago, it stands fast for ever
and ever. God cannot lie. Beloved, are any of you in trouble?
Search the Scriptures till you find a promise that suits your case; and
when you get it, do not say, "I hope that this is true." That is
an insult to your God. Believe it, believe it up to the hilt. Do
as I have seen boys do in the swimming-bath; take a header, and go
right into the stream of God's mercy; dive as deeply as you can;
there is no drowning there. These are "waters to swim in";
and the more you can lose yourself in this blessed crystal flood
of promised mercy, the better it shall be. You shall rise up out of it
as the sheep come from the washing; you shall feel refreshed
beyond measure in having cast yourself upon God. When God's promises fail, let us know of it; for some of us have lived so long on those

promises, that we do not care to live on anything else; and if they can be proved to be false, we had better give up living altogether. But we delight to know that they are all absolutely true: what God said to our fathers stands good to their children, and will stand good even to the end of time, and to all eternity.

If any of you have not been able to touch even one of these strings, I would bid you get to your knees, and cry to God, and say, " Why is it that I cannot magnify thee, O Lord ?" I should not be surprised if you discovered the reason to be that you are so big yourself. He never magnifies God who magnifies himself. Belittle yourself, and begreaten your God. Down with self to the lowest depths, and up, higher and still higher, with your thoughts of God.

Poor sinner, you that have not yet laid hold on God, there is sweet music even for you in the virgin's song. Perhaps you are saying, " I am nothing but a lump of sin and a heap of misery." Very well ; leave the lump of sin and the heap of misery, and let Christ be your all-in-all. Give yourself up to Christ. He is a Saviour ; let him do his own business. If a man sets up to be a lawyer, and I have a case in court, I should not think of giving him the case, and then afterwards go into court, and begin to meddle with it for myself. If I did, he would say, " I must drop the case if you do not let it alone." Sometimes the idea may come into your mind that you will do something towards saving yourself, and have some share in the glory of your salvation. If you do not get rid of that idea, you will be lost. Surrender yourself to Christ, and let him save you; and then afterwards he will work in you to will and to do of his own good pleasure, while you shall make melody in your heart unto the Lord, and from this harp of ten strings shall proceed such delightful melody that many shall listen with such rapture that they shall go to your Master, and take lessons in this heavenly music for themselves.

The Lord bless you, beloved, and send you away happy in him !